raising
bentley

To.
Cassie –
Cassie – Blessings to you.
Blessings to you –
Loved meeting
you... and hope
see you my you no
enjoy but wait
reading

Ca

Published by Tate Publishing & Enterprises, LLC
127 E. Trade Center Terrace | Mustang, Oklahoma 73064 USA
1.888.361.9473 | www.tatepublishing.com

Tate Publishing is committed to excellence in the publishing industry. The company reflects the philosophy established by the founders, based on Psalm 68:11,
"The Lord gave the word and great was the company of those who published it."

Published in the United States of America

ISBN: 978-1-60696-441-5
1. Inspiration: Motivational: Devotionals
2. Religion: Devotional
08.11.05

raising
bentley

Stories of Hope, Love and Perspective...

Catherine
Jodeit

TATE PUBLISHING & Enterprises

Even though Bentley has limited mobility, she has a playful spirit of joy, determination, and a willingness to please those she loves.

dedication

To Mel,
my husband–
Thank you
For your prayers,
For your help,
For your support,
For your advice,
For your patient tolerance,
And for loving me enough to
take on the unknown challenges of
Raising Bentley.
I love you, Cathy

table of contents

Part I

Part II

Part III

Part IV

Part V

Part VI

Part X

Part XI

Part XII

Part XIII

introduction

This is a story of Bentley, a yellow female lab, and the lessons God has taught us through the trials and toils of raising her. The beginning of the story and the associated devotionals are pretty much in tune with what many of you have experienced with your own pets. There might be a slightly different take on the lessons, but you will certainly recognize the experience.

Soon, the road turns. When *Bentley* was eight months old, she had a severe accident that would not only alter her life but would affect all of our family members' lives as well. For wherever we were, Bentley was, and prayers for her were on the hearts of all who were around her. We had to make some tough decisions based on some tough data. As you read through these devotionals, you will be able to track the stages we journeyed through. And for those of you reading this who have dogs, don't take for granted those four working legs and that wagging tail. Just like the saying goes, "you don't know what you have 'til it's gone!"

Bentley was given to our daughter Molly to be her steady companion when she was battling cancer. She was a perk for our whole family. Floppy paws, puppy breath, a sweet disposition, and a beautiful face. She did her job well, and Molly adored her. We all did! We have an older yellow lab named Khaki who wasn't so sure about this feisty pup invading her territory, getting all the attention, and wanting to jump and play on all accounts. They soon became fast friends though, and Bentley would definitely lively up the years to come for Khaki. But clearly Khaki was the lead dog!

When Molly was battling cancer, there were so many people who prayerfully kept up with her through e-mails, which I sent to one friend who passed them on to others who were trailing our journey. The e-mails contained prayer requests and devotionals that the Lord would put on my heart. When Molly had completed treatments and was in remission, I had thought these writings would have come to an end, but people had gotten used to them and encouraged me to continue....... so I asked God what it was that he wanted me to do?

There was just a month between Molly's freedom and Bentley's accident, and so I kept on writing, wondering, *Is God now going to teach me lessons through Bentley?* I was still trying to absorb some of the ones I learned from Molly. The answer was yes! Even though my writings were not solely about Bentley at the time, she quickly became a front burner topic, and as you will see, they make a hearty statement on her behalf. So enjoy the story through the vignettes, and while you are reading it think about what you would have done if this had come your way.

life is up:
puppy behavior

Bentley started out just like any other pup. You know that puppy smell that makes you want to stick your nose in her face and in her fur, and there is nothing quite like an expression of a pup who tilts her head when you talk to her. Her feet seldom touched the floor. And this time *this* puppy *was* allowed on the bed. She was chosen for one reason, and that reason was to be a companion to Molly, our sophomore daughter in high school, as she gallantly fought a battle with Hodgkin's Lymphoma. We already had a yellow lab named Khaki, who was fourteen years old or so. I'm not so good at keeping track of birthdays, especially the dogs.' Khaki is a terrific, calm-natured dog, but she didn't have the pep and play that would be needed to fill the gap of a perky little companion for Molly. Bentley slept a bunch as puppies do and as she grew …quickly! In step with puppy behavior; there were mistakes on the floor, she chewed anything in reach, she loved playing tug, and was always glad to give you some of those wet faced kisses. But Molly was the one she snuggled with. She was a precious pup, but aren't all pups just downright cute. Bentley was a big name for a little pup, but she soon, very soon, would grow into her name, and show us all how big she really was.

new puppy for molly
-april 18, 2006

When Molly was battling cancer, I had a precious group of friends who were on an e-mail list. I sent out devotionals and prayer requests pretty regularly to keep them informed, for it was the easiest way of communication. This was the e-mail sent that announced Bentley's arrival!

From: Cathy
To: The e-mail list of Molly's prayer warriors
Sent: Tuesday, April 18, 2006
Subject: Molly and her new pup

Another treatment downe are a quarter of the way through the chemo. God has blessed us greatly with good platelets and white blood cells intact. All is going well Mel, my husband, took Molly to pick out a new lab puppy today. There were six left in the litter. We met in Memorial Park, and after a few minutes Molly had made her choice—a yellow AKA Labrador retriever. Actually, she was more of a *white* female lab, but she fits in the yellow category. Molly chose the sweetest pup: a lot of pep, not too wild, very affectionate, and such a precious beautiful square jawed face. Molly is tickled with her choice and has named her new puppy Bentley, a name she has loved and held on to since sixth grade. She knew the day would come when she could use it. Bentley would serve as a true companion during this battle. The day had come to have a dog of her own ...named Bentley.

walking the dogs
-may 26, 2006

Molly's new dog Bentley is learning to take walks. Mel, my husband, and I walk two or three nights a week and have started taking both dogs with us. This week Mel said, "Try to keep Bentley on your right." We turned off Memorial, took her off the leash, and she followed pretty well. We have a route that we take, but because Bentley is still little we can't go the whole route.

I said to Mel, "Well, let's at least follow this first phase of our walk, so she'll know the routine.

Mel said, "It isn't important that she knows the routine it is important that she knows to stay with you and follow you." I have been walking the dogs each morning, and he's right. I have changed the routine path, but Bentley is learning to stay beside me (with only a little bit of wandering) without a leash. Khaki, our older dog, learned this a long time ago, so she never has a leash even on the busy street of Memorial.

I think you pretty much know where I'm going with this. On my walk this morning, as Bentley followed close, I thought, *God doesn't want me to get used to the same routine. He just asks that I follow him ... wherever he leads.* I get up with Bentley, feed her, wash her mat, and play with her, and she trusts me. God gets up with me, supplies my needs, and is my constant companion, and I trust him! So

when there is no leash (accountability) making me stay
on path, I too have that choice; do I follow and stay close,
or wander? Oh, I wander, but just like Bentley, I always
know my master is watching and in sight and I come
running a little faster now when I'm called.

> My sheep listen to my voice. I know them and they
> follow me.
>
> John 10:27

Praise God wherever you are and whatever situation he
has allowed you to be in. His glory will shine through!

adventure
-july 4, 2006

I love an adventure! This morning I grabbed the dogs for a walk; I knew the rain was coming, but I thought that we could make it back in time. So I asked God to let us get around the block please before the rains fell. God said no, and after we had been out for only ten minutes or so the rains came down …and not just sprinkles! I remembered this quote that I read yesterday.

An adventure is only an inconvenience rightly considered. An inconvenience is an adventure wrongly considered.
  G. K. Chesterton
  English author and mystery novelist

I thought, *This is an adventure!* I haven't been caught in the rain in ages and now here I am with two labs: Khaki, the old one, and Bentley, who is growing bigger each day. We were drenched, but the dogs were frolicking through the ditches and having a wonderful time. There was not much I could do except choose to enjoy the circumstance, and I did. It was as though we were all celebrating the day and it was truly fun. (If we would have waited just an hour, we would have missed the moment because the sun came out.) I thanked God that he did let it rain on us because he changed the everyday momentum into something new.

Oh, how I wish I could do that more often. Not the rain thing necessarily but the momentum and the attitude. For God sees joy in so much that we see drudgery in. Walking in the rain is just a reminder to change things up a little. Don't be satisfied with the same ho-hum, do something, anything, in a different way. It helps you to take a new picture of life, and you will find the joy that God has waiting.

Praise God wherever you are and whatever situation he has allowed you to be in. His glory will shine through!

chewing
-july 18, 2006

Big pup Bentley (six months, fifty pound) lost her *good dog* focus the other day and decided to take one of those red Styrofoam swimming noodles and chew it to pieces (literally). This didn't bother me much but had Mel, my husband seen it, being the orderly guy he is, he wouldn't have taken too kindly to it. So I picked up the pieces, all one hundred of them, and thought, *Is this what I do to God? Do I take my focus off of doing what is right and good and chew into pieces a worry or situation 'til I have pretty much have covered the entire thought with anxiety thus making a terrible mess of my emotions.*

If I just could have caught Bentley early, I could have avoided the clean up, and if I just could stop the thoughts early, I could avoid the wear and tear of *fret.*

So how do I stop them early? Just *substitute* one thought for another! Our minds can only have one basic thought at a time, so instead of giving into one that makes us crazy with worry or unease, think about *God* and his things on this Earth that are excellent and things in your life that are blessings!

> Finally, brothers, whatever is true, whatever is noble, whatever is right, whatever is pure, whatever is lovely, whatever is admirable—if anything is excellent or praiseworthy—think about such things.
>
> Philippians 4:8

It truly works! It takes a little time to make a habit out of it, but if you keep training your mind, you will soon be convinced that this is an easier way to live. So many of the things we worry about never even happen, and so many of the circumstances or situations we find ourselves in are things we really have no control over anyway, so why not just give them up and *let God handle them.*

Over these last few months, I have chewed and chewed some thoughts into little bitty pieces. Finally, I have had to give it up and think of the things of excellence and the many blessings I have been given. God gladly will take the worries that are swimming around in our heads, but he isn't going to yank them from us. He wants us to ask him for help and surrender what it is that has the potential of turning into a hundred pieces of worry.

Praise God wherever you are and whatever situation he has allowed you to be in. His glory will shine through!

ottoman
-august 18, 2006

I was awakened yesterday morning by the sound of Bentley tearing up something. When I entered the den I had found her chewing on the skirt of the ottoman, and she had chewed a pretty big piece of fabric right out of it. I spoke in a stern voice, popped her on the backside, and sent her outside with her tail between her legs. She tries so hard to please and truly is so sad when she gets in trouble (like most dogs, I think). When we regrouped and got going, I went in the kitchen, let the dogs back in to feed them (both dogs), and Bentley just lay on the floor with her food between her legs and didn't eat (she always eats laying down). She is the most excited about breakfast and to see her sitting so quiet and still was just pitiful. Even Mel melted, and he isn't much for any dog to do property damage. She was so sorry and knew she had messed up. I couldn't help but love her and say "Ok, but don't do it again!" It still took her a while to eat. She was really sorry!

When was the last time you messed up? Maybe it wasn't something as tangible as eating a hole in the ottoman. Maybe it was just an unkind word or an impatient response to the grocery store clerk or to your spouse or one of your kids or friends. Maybe you fought to selfishly get your way and were inconsiderate of another. Maybe you were not trustworthy or dependable or helpful when you should have been. Maybe you somehow blatantly disregarded something on God's list of laws of life (Ten Commandments)!

I can pretty much say *yes* to all of these, but the question is, "Am I really sorry? Do I humble myself before God (who already knows the issue) and truly apologize? Do I ask him not only to forgive me but also to help me to not continue to repeat the same offence? Do I ask him to change my mind and heart, which is where the real issue lies?"

If we confess our sins, he is faithful and just and will forgive us our sins and purify us from all unrighteousness.

1 John 1:9

Like Bentley, I am sorry and I feel awful when I knowingly have done something to offend someone or hurt someone or even carelessly damage property, but I know God knows my heart and knows when I truly am sorry for what I have done. He looks at me as I looked at Bentley. He loves me unconditionally and gives me another chance to do my best. Sure, I'll mess up again and so will Bentley, but for the time at hand, and all times for eternity for that matter, I am forgiven and loved. God hopefully will keep his reigns upon me and oversee my comings and goings. It is my prayer that God will *train me in his way* so that the mess-ups will be less and less as he teaches me to be more and more like him.

> Train a child in the way he should go, and when he is old he will not turn from it.
>
> Proverbs 22:6

(In this case, we are trying to train the dog.)

Praise God wherever you are and whatever situation he has allowed you to be in. His glory will shine through!

gifts
-august 25, 2006

I have a seven-month-old grandson named Blake, and a seven-month-old lab named Bentley. I never really put together how similar their toys are, but Blake has a teether that Bentley is just drooling for. Yesterday, I found a round teether that is so similar to Blake's, and I got it for Bentley! Now understand that Bentley literally loves "her cloth babies/toys" to death, but this was different—it was a large hard plastic ring with lots of colored (like that would matter) smaller rings attached around it. I gave it to Bentley, and she was so excited! I mean when I say excited; she was throwing it around, rolling on it jumping up and down with it, and bringing it to Mel and I to show it off. It was the perfect gift for Bentley, and I knew it would be because I knew Bentley.

God knows *you* and God knows *me*. He knows just what it is we need in our life and knows just what gift would send us in twirls. But do we:

1.   Recognize the gift
2.   Show how much we appreciate the gift
3.   Share the gift (Bentley would share, I think, but maybe not)

Gifts come in all different forms, but I suspect the gifts that God intends for our greatest joy are those you can't buy. Sometimes a gift of gesture, a gift of friendship, a loving spouse, precious children, grandchildren, a butterfly spotting, a rainy day, sunshine, green lights, etc. But those are all external life gifts what about inside gifts. What is it that you *do* that sends your inside into a twirl? If you can recognize that one thing, *then* you will recognize what one of your gifts is that God has given for you to use for his *glory*. It is the perfect gift for you. It will be natural …and it will be perfectly suited for your needs.

There are different kinds of gifts, but the same Spirit.

1 Corinthians 12:4

…for God's gifts and his call are irrevocable.

Romans 11:29

We have different gifts, according to the grace given us. If a man's gift is prophesying, let him use it in proportion to his faith. If it is serving, let him serve; if it is teaching, let him teach; if it is encouraging, let him encourage; if it is contributing to the needs of others, let him give generously; if it is leadership, let him govern diligently; if it is showing mercy, let him do it cheerfully.

Romans 12:6–8

Whatever your gift may be ...*use it!* And when a gift has been given ...*appreciate it!* It is my prayer that I can become as excited about little gifts that God has graciously given to me as Bentley was about this new gift that was given to her! I might not jump up and down and throw it around, but God surely will know the joy in my heart! It made me feel so good to have given her something she enjoyed so much—and it must make God smile so big when we enjoy the gifts that he hand picks for us, the inside and outside ones!

Praise God wherever you are and whatever situation he has allowed you to be in. His glory will shine through!

safety
-september 1, 2006

Yesterday, we had some floor guys come in to do some refinishing and the dogs were in. Khaki, the old, wise dog, went to her spot and lay low, Bentley, the young, mama's girl, stayed right by my side and barked an occasional threat (in her mind) towards the workers. Burney, the head guy, was just bent on getting Bentley to let her pat him. He loves dogs. But no matter how he coaxed her, she was having nothing to do with him.

We couldn't figure out if she was protecting me or staying safe. We came to the conclusion that she was staying safe.

When the unknown enters your world, where is your safe spot? Who do you go running to, and where do you hide? You go to someone who you know will protect you, someone you are familiar with and you trust and has credibility.

You are my hiding place; you will protect me from trouble and surround me with songs of deliverance.

Psalm 32:7

Keep me as the apple of your eye; hide me in the shadow of your wings.

Psalm 17:8

Rescue me from my enemies, O LORD, for I hide myself in you.

Psalm 149:9

Who are your enemies? What are your enemies? Remember the days of hide and seek, one, two, three, and ready or not, here I come! Ready or not, ups and downs of life will come! They will catch you off guard, unprepared, and sometimes just knock you off your feet.

Run to the one who will protect you. He won't always change the circumstances, but you can *count* on him to change you. He will give you courage to approach the unknown, faith to stand tall, strength to get you though the day, wisdom to make hard decisions, and comfort in knowing his loving hand is upon you.

This is the Almighty God who with his infinite wisdom, his encompassing love, and everlasting devotion cares about *you* and wants to give you *his* peace.

I will lie down and sleep in peace, for you alone, O LORD, make me dwell in safety.

Psalms 4:8

The name of the LORD is a strong tower; the righteous run to it and are safe.

Proverbs 18:10

One, two, three. Are you ready?

Praise God wherever you are and whatever situation he has allowed you to be in. His glory will shine through!

Part II

life flips to upside down: the accident

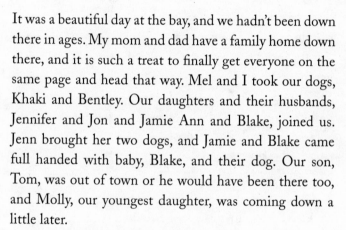

It was a beautiful day at the bay, and we hadn't been down there in ages. My mom and dad have a family home down there, and it is such a treat to finally get everyone on the same page and head that way. Mel and I took our dogs, Khaki and Bentley. Our daughters and their husbands, Jennifer and Jon and Jamie Ann and Blake, joined us. Jenn brought her two dogs, and Jamie and Blake came full handed with baby, Blake, and their dog. Our son, Tom, was out of town or he would have been there too, and Molly, our youngest daughter, was coming down a little later.

We were only spending one night, but it was something we all had looked forward to. It was the first time we had been together on an outing in a while, and it was especially freeing because it was a time to celebrate Molly's freedom from cancer. It had been a month since she had completed her treatments. There is nothing like the bay air, watching the sailboats racing in masses, and the seagulls soaring above. The smells, sounds, and sights of the bay bring such a peace to my soul …and my heart was full.

It was mid afternoon, and everyone was frolicking amidst the huge open yard facing the bay, playing, visiting, and enjoying a beautiful Labor Day holiday. The pool was the main attraction of the moment; some were in and some were out, kids, baby, dogs, but we all were around playing about outside. When all of the sudden, Bentley spotted a golden retriever at the house next door, jumped out of the pool, and bolted. None of us had any idea there was unseen danger in the neighbor's yard. She either didn't see the chain linked fence because it was camouflaged with the sky or saw it and thought she could run through it. The damage was immediate. She ran full throttle, head first, smack dab into the fence. The back of her body dropped, and she started wailing and turning in circles using her front legs. It was a horrible sight. Mel, Jennifer, Jon, and Blake went running, but Jamie and the baby stayed with me on the porch. I told Jamie she must have broken her leg. Jamie said, "Mom, go on over there." But I just couldn't!

I knew they were settling her down the best that they could and the only thing that I could do at that point was to run inside and call my Uncle Jack, who lives at the bay and knows all the spots. Susie, his wife, answered and directed me to the Emergency Vet on I-45. I went outside and told Mel that I had gotten the vet information and where we were heading and then went quickly to the car to get it ready for the transport. Mel gently picked Bentley up and carried her to the car. We had brought towels from home, so I made a mat in the way back of Mel's SUV. I stayed in the back with Bentley, and we headed to the VCA Emergency Hospital SE Calder. She whined the whole way, and I cried!

Dr. Kenneth Head was the doctor on duty. We arrived about four thirty, and he took x-rays, so many x-rays, to try to get a good look at her total spine. He gave her some drugs to settle her down, and they took pretty quickly. According to the pictures from the x-rays, there just didn't appear to be anything broken. The intense damage was to the nerves in her spinal cord. She was paralyzed from the middle of her back all the way back to her hind legs, tail, backbone, and rear end. She had no feeling whatsoever. She had done her job, as Molly's companion, for Molly was now cancer free and home free. Now what were we to do with *Bentley?*

When an accident of this kind happens, apparently, it is necessary to have surgery in the first forty-eight hours, if in fact surgery could make a difference. Since it was Labor Day, it would be hard to find a surgeon, so Dr. Head suggested that we take her to A&M and have her examined there. He would make the referral call early the following morning. Bentley was pretty drugged up mainly to keep her in a calm state and Dr. Head felt like it would be better if she stayed overnight in the office so he could watch her. We trusted him because he seemed to be hurting for this dog as much as we were. It was gut wrenching to watch this full of life, happy go lucky pup in such a serious condition, sedated and not having any idea how this was going to turn out. I know she is just a dog …but she is our dog and I know many of you know how quickly a pet can become part of a family.

We exchanged phone calls with the kids all evening, and they finally ate dinner without us. We didn't get home 'til about eleven o'clock. We were spent, all of us, and so sad! This precious full of life puppy now had a body that was in *big* trouble!

We changed the formation of the seats in Mel's car so that Bentley could lie close to the front and I could have my hand on her while I was driving to A&M. It would be about an hour and a half drive. Mel, after great deliberation, stayed at the bay with the kids. I just wanted to drive and pray by myself, so he *finally* gave in!

The folks at the A&M Veterinary Medical Teaching Hospital were waiting for us. They brought out a cart, transferred Bentley on to it, and then took her in to be examined. They offered little hope for recuperation and said there was only a five percent chance that she would ever walk again and her quality of life would doubtfully ever be good. It broke my heart. She was the sweetest tempered dog! How could we bow out on her after she had done such a wonderful job being Molly's friend and had become such a fun new family member?

I called Mel, as I sat on the outside steps of the hospital with tears just flowing and told him that they had suggested verbally that she be put down, but that I had looked at Bentley's precious face while she was in the examination room and just didn't think I could do that.

I have to say right now I adore my husband for many reasons, but one that continually comes to the surface is his ability to evaluate a situation with calmness and wisdom. This would be no exception. He said, "Let me talk to the rest of the group here at the bay and let's see if we can come up with a good decision. I'll call you back!" They prayed, I had prayed, and I know God heard our prayers. We brought her *home!*

Before leaving the hospital at A&M, I pleaded with them to tell me what to do next. I just wanted them to give me a sliver of hope. There was just not much they could do or say, but they must have seen my desperation and finally suggested that I take her on Monday to see a doctor at the Gulf Coast Veterinary Surgery, Orthopedics and Neurology (GCVS).

bentley is paralyzed
-september 4, 2006

From: Cathy
To: Prayer Warrior List
Sent: September 4, 2006
Subject: Bentley is Paralyzed

Bentley (our seven-month-old lab) ran full throttle into a cyclone fence on Sunday night while attempting to visit with the dog next door at the bay. She has severe spinal damage, and the back half of her body is paralyzed. It was suggested that we put her to sleep, but we're not quite ready to throw in the towel. God has taught me many a lesson from this four-legged friend already in her short life. Maybe having faith and trust in this life fight for her is yet another one! We took her to an emergency room last night and then drove her to A&M this morning. Please pray that somehow her body retaliates from this trauma especially knowing that her odds are so slim. They have only given her a five percent chance to ever walk again, and those are the odds God seems to take great control over!

Thank you, Cathy

The doctor's name at GCVC who we were referred to was Dr. Longshore. He was not available, but we were able to get an appointment with his associate, Dr. Abramson, a kind hearted, quiet spoken professional, who showed great empathy. She examined Bentley and pretty much said the same thing that A&M had said except, she added, "Let's bring out the *big* guns and give it our best shot up front." She put her on Prednisone, ironically the same drug that Molly had been on for five months.

And one more thing that she said that she might not have even realized she said was, "Exercise her legs as much as you can, so that *when* she walks again her muscles will not have atrophied. I was to check with her again in two weeks." Sometimes it just takes a word or two to give someone a little hope. The word she used was *when*, not *if!* It was that one little word that reminded me to never lose HOPE. For, we never know what God has planned.

impact

-september 5, 2006

Of course, God would use a dog. He knows the *impact* she could make. Look at the impact a plain old cyclone fence made on her. God knows that so many of us have been impacted in our lives by health, marriage, loss, failure, traditions, religion, fear, patriotism, success, etc. *But how?* And *why?*

How? First, by knocking us off a pedestal that was probably not on very sturdy ground in the first place. Second, by causing us to examine priorities. Third, by reaching deep into who we are rather than letting us skim by on the surface. These are some of the things that impacts have brought forth in my life.

And Why? Maybe because there is so much inside of us that has not yet been exposed, or so many gifts that have not yet been tapped. When Molly's treatment was completed and we were starting to see great light, I couldn't help but say, "Lord, I am so grateful for experiencing a walk so tender, a light so bright, a healing so awesome, and journey so dear. But where do I go from here?"

There are so many adventures that we take for granted in this life …everyday adventures. I have just experienced the medical world through our journey with Molly's cancer and now this veterinarian world is yet another piece of life that I have been called to jump into. Oh, but what I have learned from the last six months, and get to take with me.

What have you learned from the experiences that have impacted your life? What have you got in your pocket to take on your next venture? I constantly am asking, *What is it, Lord? What are you trying to teach me?* And as two friends said today in separate conversations, "Take your time." Maybe that is the lesson right now. We live in such a hurry up world, get it done today or you'll miss out tomorrow. *Take time.* Time to visit with God, time to back away from the television, time to stop and listen when your kids walk in the kitchen, time to tend to a precious four-legged friend. Just take time!

"I thank my God every time I remember you ...each of you!"

Philippians 1:3

Praise God wherever you are and whatever situation he has allowed you to be in. His glory will shine through!

dr. olby conversation
-september 5, 2006

Meanwhile, I was searching the Internet frantically for any other treatments that could help. I found that Purdue University had researched a product called PET for spinal cord injuries. It sounded perfect, but when I called Purdue, I spoke to a doctor who said it was not available for release. This was my next lead.

From: Cathy
To: Dr Olby
Sent: September 5, 2006
Subject: Bentley

Dr. Olby,

I know you are very busy, and I thank you for taking the time to read this e-mail. A researcher at Purdue University gave me your name in hopes that you might help me. My seven-month-old female lab, Bentley, has a severe spinal cord injury, which happened last Sunday evening, Sept 3. She ran full speed into a chain link fence that she didn't see going to see the dog next door. She has been to an emergency clinic then we took her to be examined at Texas A&M. They have given her a five percent chance of ever walking again. We gave this dog to my daughter in April after she was diagnosed with Hodgkin's Lymphoma phase four, in hopes that she would serve as a companion and vessel of encouragement. *She has done her job well.* Blessings and prayers have been answered, our daughter is in remission, and you can see why this is so important to our whole family. I have understood that there is a drug called OFS that you are currently working with that has shown great success with this kind of injury. Please help us if it is possible or advise us as to what, if any other, alternatives are out there that we may consider. Your kindness and time are appreciated so much. If I have to drive her to North Carolina from Houston, Texas, I will be on the road in an hour! Thank you and may God continue to bless you and the work that you are doing.

Cathy Jodeit, "Bentley's" mom

Praise God wherever you are and whatever situation he has allowed you to be in. His glory will shine through!

To: Cathy
From: Dr. Olby
Sent: September 5, 2006
Subject: Bentley

Dear Cathy,

I am sorry to hear this. We do have an OFS study ongoing in dogs that are chronically paralyzed: i.e. more than six months out from their injury and would be very happy to do everything possible to enable you to get into this trial although I hope this doesn't happen and that she does recover. Did she actually fracture her spine? Could you fax me her medical discharges including info on the tests that were run? Which neurologist did you see at Texas?

Thanks Natasha

From: Cathy
To: Dr. Olby
Sent: September 5, 2006
Subject: Bentley

Several x-rays were taken, and they found no indication of a fracture. They said damage was to the nerves. We saw Dr. Plunkett at Texas A&M who showed the x-rays to Dr. Livine and also to the radiologist. They said they felt like they could take tests, but even if tests showed damage the surgery would still only present a five percent chance of her walking again because of the nerves, so we elected not to do the CAT scan. I am sending the report now. Thank you again for your time and *reply!*

Cathy

From: Dr. Olby
To: Cathy
Sent: September 5, 2006
Subject: Bentley

Dear Cathy,

Given your commitment to getting Bentley better, you really should consider getting a workup done to see what is going on. The less than five precent chance of recovery is the number we give for traumatic injuries, particularly if the vertebrae are fractured or displaced. As this does not appear to be the case based on radiographs, you should be sure that there is nothing more treatable even if this is unlikely and you need advise on rehabilitation to maximize her ability to recover, even if the chances are very low. I know an excellent neurologist in Dallas if you need a referral.

Regards, Natasha Olby

bentley status
-september 6, 2006

From: Cathy
To: Prayer Warriors
Sent: September 6, 2006
Subject: Bentley

We only stayed for a doctor's visit and evaluation at A&M. We were there for several hours but I brought her home yesterday. Today, after conferring with many out of state folks who are researchers for paralysis, we ended up, after several referrals, at Gulf Coast Vet. Dr. Adamson, a poised, sensitive, totally thorough lady, chose to get off the regular protocol and bring out the big guns now instead of waiting for swelling to go down etc. Bentley, who has tracked Molly in so many funny ways, will now be taking Prednisone, a drug that Molly was on for four months, and hopefully and prayerfully she will continue to track Molly with success. Bentley's body will have to learn how to network around dead nerves and process a new nerve route so that she can have the possibility of walking again. It is a very long shot, but it is a shot, and I suspect God is a terrific aim!

May God *impact* you today as he shows you the many blessings you have and the adventures he has chosen to help you be all that *he* knows you can be!

Praise God wherever you are and whatever situation he has allowed you to be in. His glory will shine through!

handicapped
-september 7, 2006

Two thoughts.

One on the side of the caregiver—Upon reflection after spending three days with this "down" dog and her handicapped condition; we have to hoist her with a towel to help her get outside, bring her food and water to her, play with only frontal motion and position her on a soft pallet as we go from room to room. It has made me think of all of the people who have had and still do have parents or children with limited mobility and ability. I see you and often hear your stories, but 'til I have experienced it (just like anything else) I really didn't understand the time, the love, the commitment, the patience, the resourcefulness, the energy (mental and physically) that go into it. I still don't—this is a dog—but it sure has made me look with question and compassion and appreciation for all of you who are so dedicated to someone who you care for with your heart and their body. You are to be commended as you have and are serving with great fortitude. God sent Christ to serve us, and what a terrific imitation those of you who help others so unselfishly are to those of us who are watching and taking notice.

The greatest among you will be your servant.

Matthew 23:11

...but made himself nothing, taking the very nature of
a servant, being made in human likeness.

Philippians 2:7

The other—the side of the patient—I look at Bentley.
She is the sweetest dog; she is in no pain, totally alert,
wants to play tug, is so appreciative when she receives
any attention, demands nothing, and waits her turn to be
fed and watered, and is content if someone is just in the
room.

Now, I know this is pushing it, but there is a lesson
for me here and maybe for you, too. We were born in a
pretty restless selfish state (sin), and we are called to be
dependent on Christ!

Those who live according to the sinful nature have their
minds set on what that nature desires; but those who
live in accordance with the Spirit have their minds set
on what the Spirit desires.

Romans 8:5

Am I appreciative for the many blessings that have been
bestowed upon me? Am I content to be in the spot God

has designated for me? Am I demanding of God or do I *wait* patiently for his hand to guide my life? Do I smile when I am paralyzed by what life has sent my way? This is a note sent to me by a friend and I think it holds so true.

Our dog, Bess, serves as a constant reminder to me of God's love to us and convicts me as to how I should be with the Lord. She stays at our feet and looks to us for every decision. How we should do the same with the Lord!

God has got my attention, no doubt, and it is not with a loud blast but with the gentle sigh …of Bentley! God is Good!

Praise God wherever you are and whatever situation he has allowed you to be in. His glory will shine through!

equipment
-september 8, 2006

It is hard to walk Khaki, the old dog, and leave Bentley at home …so to compensate, I got out the big wagon and loaded Bentley up …just for an outing! We just went to the next street, and on the way back, the wagon broke. The front axle lost a nut and the axle just separated from the wagon. . Who knows where the nut was? There I was with a half paralyzed dog and a broken wagon, *and I thought I looked silly with the dog in the wagon.* I put the broken part in the wagon with Bentley, lifted it so that the back wheels were the main support, and started walking backwards, pulling the wagon, and holding Bentley's collar to keep her from falling out because of the tilt. I should have checked the wagon before I left, but who would have thought to check? Mel would have! He always is about preventing problems before they come. It wasn't strong and neither was I, so I prayed and asked God for some of his strength!

[The Armor of God] Finally, be strong in the LORD and in his mighty power.

Ephesians 6:10

Two cars stopped; first, a lady with her daughter (about eleven), who parked and walked down the sidewalk on Memorial to meet us and help us, but I didn't really know how to delegate help so I told her thank you, but we were okay, and very sympathetically they left, after loving on Bentley. Looking back, God was listening. We walked a little further and a second truck stopped, it was a guy from Center Point Energy. He rolled down his window as he was traveling on Memorial and said how much further are you going? I told him just half a block, and he smiled and said okay and drove slowly off. Before I knew it, this guy had parked on my street and had come to meet us! He said, "I just have to pull this the rest of the way for you." Graciously, I accepted. I studied the axle while walking and remembered that my son, Tom, had brought in the axle of the smaller wagon, that he had found in the garage the night we got home with Bentley, thinking that we could use it someway, but it was without the handle. Looking at this front axle in my hand, it was larger and with a handle and maybe it could be a base for Bentley's rear on rollers. God never wastes anything, even a breakdown! My mind was rolling …literally!

When they had all had enough to eat, he said to his disciples, "Gather the pieces that are left over. Let nothing be wasted.

John 6:12

I found out this guy's name was Pat, and I said, "I know you have a full schedule."

And he said, "Yes ma'am, but you can never be too busy to stop and help someone who needs it." I did need help. I was a little stubborn to admit it, but I did.

> And in the church God has appointed first of all apostles, second prophets, third teachers, then workers of miracles, also those having gifts of healing, those able to help others, those with gifts of administration, and those speaking in different kinds of tongues.
>
> 1 Corinthians 12:28

When God gives you the opportunity to make a difference in someone's life, but your schedule is tight ... do it anyway!

You will be blessed:

One. For the time you took. God will honor it.

Two. The person helped will somehow (even if they don't know Christ) know that help came when it was needed.

Three. You never know when a kindness plants a seed from our Lord.

I told Pat, the Center Point guy, about my idea for the wheels, and said, "See God never wastes anything." He replied, "No, ma'am, he doesn't. I just wake up each morning thankful to be alive. The rest is just gravy."

I lift up my eyes to the hills, where does my help come from? My help comes from the LORD, the Maker of heaven and earth.

Psalm 121:1

P.S. Seeing how hard Molly laughed when I told her this story was priceless! It had to be a funny sight! And it fit right in to my "Lucy" adventures.

Praise God wherever you are and whatever situation he has allowed you to be in. His glory will shine through!

let go
-september 11, 2006

Bentley is restricted on the outside, but she seems to maintain her quest for play on the inside. So we gave her a chance to play tug, a game she loved before the accident. She loved to play tug of war with a rope that has knots tied at either end. She would play, planting her front feet, gritting her teeth, tossing her head from side to side, and then reeling her head back and forth. She just loved the game. When you say, "Let *go*," she just would grip it harder because she wanted to win. Once she wins though, it isn't fun anymore, so she would plead with you through those big brown eyes to play once more, and I would; it would go on and on! She definitely has limited mobility, but she still loved the hold …and the attention.

Is there something you are holding tightly to? Do you just plant you feet, grit your teeth, and hold on no matter how hard the fight? Do you just want to win or maybe control the situation? Do you know *whom* you are tugging with? Satan wants you to keep up the fight when God says, "*let go*." Do you keep coming back for more and taking *it* (whatever "it" may be) back over and over again?

[Jesus Comforts His Disciples] Do not let your hearts be troubled. Trust in God; trust also in me.

John 14:1

How long must I wrestle with my thoughts and every day have sorrow in my heart? How long will my enemy triumph over me?

Psalm 13:2

This happens to me so often. I let go, then take it back again, let go, and then take it back again. God must be so amused seeing me wiggle back and forth knowing that if I would just let him have it, I mean really let him have it, there would be such peace in my heart!

Peace I leave with you; my peace I give you. I do not give to you as the world gives. Do not let your hearts be troubled and do not be afraid.

John 14:27

I know God is trying to mold me and remind me to "let go" of whatever it is I'm holding onto because:

1. Worrying about it is just a waste of energy. God will do what is best.

2. God already has the solution. He sees the whole picture. I only see a tiny glimpse.

3. It really comes down to *trust*. *Who* do I trust more, God or self? (And I'm learning that my *self* just doesn't have the answers.)

Please, God, help me to *not* play tug of war with circumstances that I have no control over, and even the ones that I think I do. Remind me to include *you* in on decisions. Let me be able to "let go" and release the tug peacefully, *Trusting* in *you* and your *timing!*

Praise God wherever you are and whatever situation he has allowed you to be in. His glory will shine through!

butterflies

-september 12, 2006

Yesterday, I took Bentley outside for a while just so she could enjoy the grass and try to eat flying bugs while lying down. Mel has planted some flowers out front that seem to attract butterflies. I was watching as two of them, a monarch and a black one, hovered over the flowers. I watched their wings. The monarch fluttered very deliberately and methodically, and the black one had wings that were going full throttle, no time to waste. They were both about the same size, but going about their chore at different speeds. Each flying from one flower to the next but pursuing the same goal: food. In some ways, we are like those butterflies: some of us move faster than others, we look a little different and we are just busy—non-stop. In some ways, we aren't: our pursuits aren't quite so simplified.

In our kitchen, I have this sign that reads "Simplify, Simplify, Simplify," and as I get older, it seems like simplicity is a factor worth pursuing. It is so easy to fill life up with non-essentials and let the really good stuff get squeezed out. We get caught up in the who's and where's and what's and why's instead of being grateful for moments and memories and mighty works of our mighty God.

There is a grace and poise in which the mere existence of butterflies exudes. They are beautiful! God made these creatures and they bring such joy and wonder if we take the time to stop long enough to notice them. Remember that butterflies didn't start out being so beautiful and graceful; there was a transformation. We too, are being transformed.

> From the fullness of his grace we have all received one blessing after another.
>
> John 1:16

> Do not conform any longer to the pattern of this world, but be transformed by the renewing of your mind. Then you will be able to test and approve what God's will is—his good, pleasing and perfect will
>
> Romans 12:12

I pray that God will continue to transform you and me into a likeness that would be representative of a humble adopted child of a king. I pray that each time I catch a glimpse of a butterfly that I will be reminded of the blessings of God, small and grand and in between and I will be willing to be changed by the holy hand of God.

I know *God* is watching and waiting as each day begins, to see if I choose to include him in my day! He takes time to notice. For it is with God that my day will be complete—and without his presence I am always longing for something or somebody else and never seem to be satisfied. What is your choice for your day? Mine is to have a wise dear friend by my side: *God!*

Praise God wherever you are and whatever situation he has allowed you to be in. His glory will shine through!

too perky to keep down

We have only been caring for Bentley for a week or so. The first few nights we let her sleep in a crate, but the mess was more trouble than the transport. So we decided to let her sleep in our bathroom each night ...and we would get up, express (help her to go to the bathroom) her on puppy pads in the middle of the night and load her up the next morning on her rolling flat bed, and pull her to the kitchen where breakfast would begin. Each day, I would wonder what is going on inside of her body and if she really is ever going to be able to walk again, and then I would quickly replace that thought with *hope*. And look forward to that hope.

We had to figure out a way to transport Bentley to and fro when nighttime came because she was just too heavy to carry. So I searched in the garage and found an old side to one of those elfa metal desks, from the container store, leaning up against a wall, and took it to Home Depot. There we found a flat square furniture dolly that we could connect to the shelf with metal brackets. The brackets had an arched area that fit right over the metal frame and then we were able to screw them into the wooden base of the dolly. We had figured out how to make a rolling bed for Bentley! But it needed something soft on top, so we bought an outdoor chair pad from the garden center and secured it by using the ties on the pad. It was perfect. We tied a thick old yellow sash, from my son Tom's former Karate days, to the bed and we were ready for transport.

Bentley knew the drill and would try to help by lifting her front legs, we would lift her rear, and she would flop and wait to be escorted to her bed ...then we would repeat the same drill to bring her back to the kitchen. If she was in pain, we never knew it, for she never cried or whined ...or winced. I think she was just paralyzed and felt nothing.

chariot

-september 13, 2006

Mel, my husband, made Bentley a chariot so that she could go walking. It is pretty cool little cart made out of PVC pipe, a couple of old lounge chair wheels, and two large eye screws to attach her harness to and two lambs cloth straps to hold up her hind legs. The wheels do the coasting for her hind limbs while the front legs do the walking. Bentley was a little reserved at the idea at first, but after trusting us and trying it, she realized that the assistance would give her the strength and mobility that would help make her independent. (I know this is a big thought for a dog, but she's a big dog.)

How many times has God offered you help, and because of reservation, you declined? If you did it God's way, you might have to give something up; walk a new walk, avert the same *old* way or step out of a comfort zone that is "*oh*" so familiar. God's way gives us mobility to be who we were created to be. He gives us the props to help us learn a new way, and to look at things, people and situations from a new perspective. His chariot is there for the offering, but he is not going to force the ride.

Bentley proudly galloped down the street in her new wheels; reluctant at first, for sure, but after a short introduction was ready to get after it 'cause Khaki (the old dog) was in her sight and in the lead! I bet there *has* been someone in your life who has been a leader—a pastor, a friend, someone you have watched from the outside. God has sent each of us a someone to follow who represents *his* way and his example. Though reluctance may have a stronghold, just get on God's chariot—take it slow and give the wheels that God has provided you with a chance to help pick up the dragging humdrum of life. Roll with confidence and peace knowing that God works through and around our inadequacies. He doesn't want us to be stuck in the same spot …like Bentley was. The chariot is a means to God's end. Who are you going to follow? Who will be your lead?

"Come, follow me," Jesus said, "and I will make you fishers of men."

Matthew 4:19

Then Jesus said to his disciples, "If anyone would come after me, he must deny himself and take up his cross and follow me."

Matthew 16:24

[The Validity of Jesus' Testimony] When Jesus spoke again to the people, he said, "I am the light of the world. Whoever follows me will never walk in darkness, but will have the light of life."

John 8:12

Praise God wherever you are and whatever situation he has allowed you to be in. His glory will shine through!

life jacket
-september 15, 2006

They say that people get bored, I think dogs do too! To try to keep Bentley active, I bought her a life jacket, strapped it around her tummy, and put her in the pool. She can swim with her front paws but has a hard time keeping up with the weight in the back and she starts to sink without help. If she would have accepted the floatation devise without reservation and without putting up such a fight, it may have been successful …but her confidence level with trying new things isn't so strong. So, if she was to be in the pool, she would rather be in someone's arms rather than dependent on something that she was not familiar with.

Are you trying to carry the weight of life on your shoulders? Do you need some help? Maybe a life jacket. The thing about a life jacket is it surrounds you, lifts you, and keeps you afloat. God is so available to be wrapped around you, to lift you, and to keep you afloat. He is a life jacket with a lifetime guarantee. He knows when you jump into the waters of day-to-day living you are going to need some help. Some encouragement, some comfort, some peace, some joy, some direction, some patience, some wisdom. God is dependable but just like a life jacket; you have to put him on for him to fulfill his purpose in you and for you.

To be made new in the attitude of your minds; and to put on the new self, created to be like God in true righteousness and holiness. Therefore each of you must put off falsehood and speak truthfully to his neighbor, for we are all members of one body.

Ephesians 4:23–25

Next time you feel like you are sinking reach for God. He is the greatest lifesaver of all! You can always count on him to be available, to help you if you are sinking, and to hold you up when the weight of life seems to be pulling you under. He is the someone …the familiar someone … who you can trust …not just some devise that has been manufactured to keep you from going under. He has been tested and proved to be a true source of help in troubled waters. Reach for him …with confidence!

Praise God wherever you are and whatever situation he has allowed you to be in. His glory will shine through!

moving out of bed

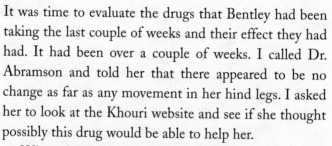

It was time to evaluate the drugs that Bentley had been taking the last couple of weeks and their effect they had had. It had been over a couple of weeks. I called Dr. Abramson and told her that there appeared to be no change as far as any movement in her hind legs. I asked her to look at the Khouri website and see if she thought possibly this drug would be able to help her.

When the dead end with Purdue University was hit with Dr. Olby, I kept looking diligently for anything … anything that would give us any hope. I even investigated several Web sites, but I was not confident enough in the legitimacy of their claims so I let it go. I had called Dr. Charles Khouri who I had found through the internet who had accidentally found a treatment for dogs with spinal cord injuries, and spoke to him, but it seemed like the dogs he had worked with had more of an arthritic problem than a spinal cord injury.

I mean I was looking for anything. She called back and said no that she didn't think that the drug would have an effect on Bentley's spinal injury. I asked if there was anything, anything else that could possibly help her. There was a pause and then she said, "We have an acupuncture doctor at this clinic and I really don't know what kind of experience she has had with this sort of injury …but I think that would have more chance than any of your other options." So, she made the referral call and our first appointment was September 26. When I told Mel, I was going to try acupuncture you can imagine his hesitancy. I was hesitant too because acupuncture just sounded like voodoo but I had run out of options. Mel said, "Go ahead and try it, Cathy."So we were off to a new doctor and a tiny ray of new hope!

Her name was Dr. Dee Harris. What a sweetheart and she adored Bentley right from the beginning. I told her that as far as I could tell, there had been no change since Dr. Abramson examined her last week, and she said, "Well, let's take a look." She did and came back and said there has been a change. Bentley does have some "deep pain" that was non-existent on her last exam. I was so grateful. Finally, something positive even if it was only a glimmer!

Dear Lord, Please Keep your hand on this big pup!

spot change
-september 18, 2006

Bentley's basic condition has no visible changes. Though the doctor could see internal ones, she still was paralyzed in her hind legs, but her attitude had changed! The first week she stayed pretty close to her mat in the kitchen and watched everything and everybody. Very quiet, very solemn, and very lethargic. It broke my heart every time I looked at her, but I kept thinking, *At least she is alive and we don't know what God has planned.* In a few short days, she started coming alive and her personality was emerging again. She is like one of those sea lions. She uses her front legs and drags herself wherever she wants to go. She made it around the island in the kitchen, through the dining room, and almost up the hall before she was restrained.

What is different? She is *determined* to not let this stop her. Her mind has been *set*! She is motivated by curiosity, desire, wanting to be active, and wanting to be by me (I figure I am the security blanket) ! Attitude check? What is motivating you? What have you set your mind on? Are you determined to not be confined by personal limitations? Are you ready to take on new challenges? Somebody called young labs "fearless." They are. She is! I want to be fearless. Fearless in my faith, fearless in my attitude, fearless in my walk with God.

Oswald Chambers said in his devotional on September 15, "the greatest spiritual crisis comes when a person has to *move a little further* on in his faith than the beliefs he has already accepted" and "not be afraid to look at things from God's perspective."[1]

If you seem to be stuck in the same spot, change your attitude. Be motivated by the blessings that God has already given you and the life plans he has made *just* for you. Set your mind to looking at things from God's perspective instead of how the world is twisting your priorities. In order to grow, I have to be willing to get out of my comfortable spot with God and look for the *new* adventures that he has offered. My curiosity needs to lead me to inquire and ask "what does God want me to do?" and my devotion, my true devotion, should be to God not anybody else or anything else.

I am saying this for your own good, not to restrict you, but that you may live in a right way in undivided devotion to the LORD.

1 Corinthians 7:35

You were taught, with regard to your former way of life, to put off your old self, which is being corrupted by its deceitful desires; to be made new in the attitude of your minds; and to put on the new self, created to be like God in true righteousness and holiness.

Ephesians 4:22–24

Many are the plans in a man's heart, but it is the LORD's purpose that prevails.

Proverbs 19:21

Bentley's limitations have not stopped her from pursuing new territory - I have to ask what is stopping me?

Praise God wherever you are and whatever situation he has allowed you to be in. His glory will shine through!

tail wagging
-september 19, 2006

I know so many of you reading this have dogs, and you see them every day and feed them and take them out, but when was the last time you noticed their tail wagging? It's not that *it hasn't wagged;* it is that *you haven't noticed.* Bentley *can't* wag her tail, but you can see expression of that *tail wagging* in her eyes. It just makes me think how much of the everyday, ordinary things of life that we take for granted and don't take time to notice.

It's the little things: your car starting, hot water, a warm bed, dinner, being able to walk, just waking up each morning. We don't think too much about them. We just expect them. As it is with God. He's always around just watching patiently on the sidelines, waiting to be invited to be a part of your life, but *oh* too often he goes unnoticed not to mention unappreciated. (You can't appreciate someone's talents if you don't know what they are.) You don't know how skilled the player is 'til you give him a chance to play. We seem to just expect *God* to be there when something tough happens and we need some help, and don't let him train with us before the *Big Game* hits.

I pray today that God continually will remind me of his presence in everything, all the ordinary stuff, so that one day when he comes to this Earth, I will not only go with him at that moment but will be filled with his blessings during ordinary days that he gave me when I was on this Earth.

You also must be ready, because the Son of Man will come at an hour when you do not expect him.

Luke 12:40

Having God beside me each day *is* a tail wagging experience, and I pray that God will let it show in my eyes even if my tail doesn't wiggle.

I first have to take *notice* of *his presence* especially in the small stuff!

Praise God wherever you are and whatever situation he has allowed you to be in. His glory will shine through!

hurry up and slow down
-september 20, 2006

I like getting things done quick, not a bunch of talking about it or planning for it or measuring or reading, just get it done! Then I think about Molly and the homework we did before we decided on a protocol for her cancer. It took time, but it was the right decision. Then I thought about Bentley. A&M suggested that we put her to sleep and that her chances were only five percent to be able to walk again. We decided to wait, still are, and still doing homework. Looking back, so many of my mistakes are because I was trying to do things in a big hurry. (This is when you are expecting an example; nope, too many to pick from.) Quick fixes, so many times, are just band-aids; a cover for what really needs tending to. Real fixes take time, lots of time!

We so easily get frustrated with ourselves or others because we mess up, do the wrong thing, say the wrong thing, and act the wrong way. God is never in a hurry, and he is not in a hurry to mold us into his likeness. He takes it *slow* so what we learn will stick and he can build on it. He is pursuing a good foundation that has been laid by *him* not by man. I have spent a bunch of time at home the last few months. It is pretty quiet here. Not much for TV and I forget about turning on music, but it has forced me to slow down and look at life from a very rich standpoint: God's. When you are not rushing to the next appointment or luncheon or meeting and having to decide what you are going to wear and the getting ready part, you are left with a pretty simple setting. Quiet time with God.

Think for a minute about the disciples and the many times they just casually walked with God. Think of the conversations; what they *heard* what they *learned,* what they *saw* just by watching the way *God* handled situations and people. When I am in a hurry up state, I know I am missing some good lessons and sweet whispers that God has offered. Sometimes I just need to *be still.* Remember when the storms came and the disciples were so scared and He (Jesus) got up, rebuked the wind, and said to the waves, "Quiet! Be still!" (Mark 4:39). Then the wind died down and it was completely calm.

I am sure there are so many times God has wanted to say to me *"Quiet! Be still"* so he could pour into me *his* calm. God is trying to teach me to *take time.* It might not happen at the blink of an eye, but for now he's peeked my interest. By *his* choice God has turned my hurry up state into a hunker down state, and I have to say it is really pretty peaceful.

If God has put you in a quiet spot, savor it. Let God pour his thoughts upon you …and into you.

The grace of our LORD was poured out on me abundantly, along with the faith and love that are in Christ Jesus.

1 Timothy 1:14

He saved us, not because of righteous things we had done, but because of his mercy. He saved us through the washing of rebirth and renewal by the Holy Spirit, whom he poured out on us generously through Jesus Christ our Savior, so that, having been justified by his grace, we might become heirs having the hope of eternal life.

Titus 3:5–7

If you are in hurry up mode, change gears every now and then, even if it is just for comparison.

Be still, and know that I am God.

Psalm 46:10

What if the words were changed to hurry down and slow up? Time is a valuable commodity. Who and what are you spending yours with?

Praise God wherever you are and whatever situation he has allowed you to be in. His glory will shine through!

curb jumping
-september 22, 2006

We live in a society of extremes: too much, too little, too short, too late, too shallow, too deep, too right, too left, etc. Where do we go to find balance? Bentley has grown very accustomed to her new wheels. We take a little walk several times a day, and she is just as perky as can be trotting down the street. But this morning the neighbor's sprinklers were on, and Bentley forgot that she has some limitations and she tried to jump that curb and sail into the water. Didn't work! *She lost her balance.* The cart tumbled in slow motion, and she just rolled right on down to the ground, a little stunned but ready to get up and go again without much thought or damage

When was the last time you lost your balance, not just physically, but in life? Were you too heavy in one area and or did you maybe run out of time in another area? Has juggling family, time, work, friends, and hobbies just turned into one big tangle of life? Have you jumped right into something or chased something that you really weren't equipped to handle or maybe didn't even want to handle, but you submitted to an outside pressure? Sometimes the choices that are offered by others or even the ones we think we are choosing for the right reasons just don't work. God is so available to help us pick and choose so that our lives remain in balance. He wants *his* plan to remain in *our* focus, but we have to realize he does *have* a plan. Here we are in a new season. The days have been beautiful, the sun shining, a hint of breeze and what a great time to shake off some of the weights that have tilted our scales of a balanced life. We have to ask God to help us figure out what to keep and what to let go remembering that *good* is not always best. Just because we are doing something for God doesn't necessarily mean that God was the one who asked us to do it!

For I know the plans I have for you," declares the LORD, "plans to prosper you and not to harm you, plans to give you hope and a future.

Jeremiah 29:11

How magnificent is grace! How malignant is guilt! How sweet are the promises! How sour is the past! How precious and broad is God's love! How petty and narrow are man's limitations! How refreshing is the Lord!
Chuck Swindoll[2]

I will refresh the weary and satisfy the faint.

Jeremiah 31:25

Dear God, if I'm going curb jumping help me remember to ask you first if this is what you have equipped me to do! Thank you . Amen

Praise God wherever you are and whatever situation he has allowed you to be in. His glory will shine through!

tweaking

-september 25, 2006

Isn't it fun to just get going on a project and finally have it finished (so you think)? Then one more glance sends an urgent message to your brain to tweak it just a little more, and it will be great. Sometimes you have to try it out and then stand back, get a new perspective and look at it again. *So it is* with Bentley's chariot. After a few test drives, there are a few adjustments that will make it just right for a sturdy pull. It works just fine but a couple of changes could make it even better.

So it is with these devotionals. I write them and they are just fine but after thinking about them for a while God puts on my heart a few changes. I have to let them simmer before I know where to make the changes. It starts with a gradual readjustment in my mind.

And *so it is* with life! It starts with a gradual readjustment in your mind. What does God want to do to you and through you to tweak his creation? Maybe it is dealing with forgiveness, or kindness, unkindness, or understanding towards someone else. Look a little harder at the grocery store clerk, the people who are filing their car up at the same time you are, the construction guys on I-10, the people in your workplace, or the park. Everybody has a story. What could you do to tweak yours? Maybe I could simplify or organize (yikes) what I have been blessed with or pursue an interest that God has caused to brew within or maybe he just might want me to spend a little more time with *him* in prayer, in his word, in his shadow, in his light.

Things might be going smooth or your road might be filled with potholes, but God knows the road you are on. He wants you to move over and let him drive, for he will tweak the journey with perseverance, with joy, with peace, with wisdom, and all with the guidance of his loving hand. His way is better than ours and seeing what's going on in the light sure proves out over finding your way in the dark. Just think about traveling on a dark road at night—can't see the bends of the road, can't see the signs, no warning when something is going to jump out in your path and no help around if you need it. He knows the way and will tweak your travel. *He is the way!*

Jesus answered, "I am the way and the truth and the life. No one comes to the Father except through me."

John 14:6

I saw that wisdom is better than folly, just as light is better than darkness.

Ecclesiastes 2:13

Through *his* process of sanctification God's goal is to make us better; through trials and adversity, through sorrow and pain, through unmerited blessings, through unknown territories, through sunshine and joy, but always *through his* sieve.

> And we, who with unveiled faces all reflect the LORD's glory, are being transformed into his likeness with ever-increasing glory, which comes from the LORD, who is the Spirit.
>
> 2 Corinthians 3:18

May God *tweak* where I am weak.

Praise God wherever you are and whatever situation he has allowed you to be in. His glory will shine through!

SORROW

-september 27, 2006

When I see someone crying, it just tears my heart to pieces. I think a lot of folks feel pretty much like that! I was at the vet again on Tuesday. They had taken Bentley in, and I was in the waiting room—a young girl came to the desk to pay her bill and the receptionist said, "I am so sorry."

She said, "Thank you." Tears were rolling down her face, she sat for a minute in the waiting room and then she was called to the back—a few minutes later she returned with a small box caring the remains of a beloved pet. *Oh, God, I have to say something to this lady. I don't even know her, but I do know she is hurting so bad and needs a friend. She is all alone.*

Tell her that if she hurts that bad then she must have loved so much and surely her precious cat knew of that love by the way she was treated. What a wonderful life that cat had having her as caretaker. Tell her that you will pray that I shall comfort her and ask her name!

To many of you, you might think this is over the top but I have learned over the years to recognize it when God puts something on my heart to do …then just do it without question and without reservation. So I did it, I followed her down the hall patted her back and told her the thoughts that I felt God had put on my heart! With a tender face marked with sincere appreciation, she said, "Thank you for your words. I know."

I think all of us can relate to sorrow …some have experienced much greater sorrow than others but we all know the deep tug of anguish that seems to flood our heart gates. Perhaps with the loss of a parent, a child, a sibling, a dear friend or someone you looked up to and admired. It is a feeling down deep in your gut and it is gripping. God knows. He has experienced it first hand and not only did his son die but he authorized it! That takes grief into an unyielding pit of sorrow. God understands the heartache. He empathizes with it. Sometimes he uses people to send a message, sometimes, it is through his word, or a song, or just the sight of something he knows would lift your spirits. But God is with you when those dark times overshadow any joy that you may have had.

My soul is weary with sorrow; strengthen me according to your word.

Psalm 119:28

O my Comforter in sorrow, my heart is faint within me.

Jeremiah 8:18

I hesitated including this story because it seems so gloomy, but the truth is that these times are going to hit each one of us—not just once or twice either and when they do, be prepared to *ask* God for comfort. Be prepared to ask him as a dear friend, not just in relation to someone you have heard about or read about. When you see someone hurting and their heart is just broken to pieces, don't be timid ...be the light that God has given you to be! Say something, anything, to let them know that you are sorry for their pain and that they are not alone. It is the alone part that just hits us in the stomach. Many times God is the one who shows up when no one else is around. Be their reminder that God is near—always!

Comfort, comfort my people, says your God.

Isaiah 40:1

Blessed are those who mourn, for they will be comforted.

Matthew 5:4

...who comforts us in all our troubles, so that we can comfort those in any trouble with the comfort we ourselves have received from God.

2 Corinthians 1:4

Life is being lived all around us. It is not just about yours or mine, and we are called to share joys and sorrows with those God has put in our path. You may or may not *know* them, but God does. And he's counting on each of us to be his arms for hugs, his ears to hear, and his eyes to see. Be Bold in the name of the Lord, for it must please him so for us to realize his presence and pass it on to someone in need.

Praise God wherever you are and whatever situation he has allowed you to be in. His glory will shine through!

Part V

progress is showing

Bentley is getting stronger and stronger in those front legs for she is desperate to get around and knows that that is her only measure for independence. We are still house bound though …but we do take outings to the front yard and on our street. Only God knows what is to come, and all we can do at this point is to have faith that God is watching and somehow, someway God's plan is being worked out into Bentley's life, our lives, and even God might be making a difference in someone else's through some of these lessons. We just have to be patience and wait …no matter how slow the progress seems to be … At least it is progress.

hope
-september 28, 2006

Hope is such a small word, but it holds such encouragement when spoken. I took Bentley to the vet on Monday with seemingly no progress. She was examined, and I was told that she has made remarkable improvement and *deep pain,* which was not present three weeks ago is now apparent. (Seldom is there ever a change.) She is moving both hips and can stand (with help getting her feet planted) for several minutes. Oh, what a praise and such an encouragement to keep on going. It has renewed our strength.

God has extended his *hand* of encouragement to you and to me. That nail scarred hand. He gave us *hope* then and it is available to all of us through all of time. For we saw what happened in spite of a tragedy; through *his tragedy* we saw *his glory.* When life is tough and things look bleak and *moving* is just too hard there is still *hope,* that little word with an enormous potential to adjust attitude.

Be strong and take heart, all you who hope in the LORD.

Psalm 31:24

But those who hope in the LORD will renew their strength. They will soar on wings like eagles; they will run and not grow weary, they will walk and not be faint.

Isaiah 40:31

Hope is a little flicker, that spark, that induces *thought* of victory through our mighty God. God wants us not only to recognize victory but expect it. There are times when life's demands get such a grip on us that we can hardly move. We sit stymied in a state of oblivion unable to participate in day to day living …'til God sends a vessel carrying *his* seed of *hope* right to the port of our soul. For it is *hope,* that expression of looking forward instead of backward and engaging in life rather than drowning in the floods of dismay, that will be enough to sustain us and encourage us. Be encouraged. For God loves you and me so much. May *his* joy and peace enter our hearts through the *hope* he has given us through his son Jesus.

For I know the plans I have for you," declares the LORD, "plans to prosper you and not to harm you, plans to give you hope and a future.

Jeremiah 29:11

Be joyful in hope, patient in affliction, faithful in prayer.

Romans 12:12

May the God of hope fill you with all joy and peace as you trust in him, so that you may overflow with hope by the power of the Holy Spirit.

Romans 15:13

Now faith is being sure of what we hope for and certain of what we do not see.

Hebrews 11:1

There have been many prayers for Bentley. God's mighty hand is even upon a beloved pet. She is ready to keep on keeping on, and it is such a reminder to me to do the same—in all circumstances.

Today, may God use the seed of encouragement which he has sent and plant *his hope* within your heart. May you be convinced and convicted today more than ever that God is real and he is standing patiently at the door of you heart waiting to be invited to share your day. His *hope* is that you will extend the invitation to him to join you! For God is willing and ready to equip you for the challenges he knows to come as well as the blessings that he has proclaimed.

Praise God wherever you are and whatever situation he has allowed you to be in. His glory will shine through!

route

-october 5, 2006

Well, it has almost been a month since Bentley had her accident. There has been improvement, and I am faithful that God will heal her. Things had to change at our house when this happened ...we had to change. As Bentley's body is rerouting her network of nerve commands, we have had to reroute our schedules, our routines, and our responsibilities to be able to care for her and tend to her needs. The "she's just a dog" thing has pretty much vanished. It is all about adjustment, and adjustment takes time! You try different techniques at different times with different tools to most efficiently accomplish the goal at hand. Finally, you find something or some way that works, and you are delighted with the success no matter how big or small.

We have to make adjustments in life too, everyday. Some adjustments are long term—some short—but we are pushed to alter a way of life, a habit, a response, a route etc. Just look at what I-10 has done to force us to alter a route, but we get used to it, know the drill, and incorporate it into our time and destination expectations. Adjustment is a required change to make something better. What changes are being required of you? Are you grumbling and complaining or are you gracefully holding your tongue, putting a smile on your face, and trying to find *the better way* or *be the better way?*

> For it is God who works in you to will and to act
> according to his good purpose. Do everything without
> complaining or arguing, so that you may become
> blameless and pure, children of God without fault in a
> crooked and depraved generation, in which you shine
> like stars in the universe.
>
> Philippians 2:13–15

God has called us to do all things without fussing and
arguing about them. To do that requires a supernatural
force within that holds a sword to the throat of bitterness
as grace humbly glides forth. Whatever I do, if I do it
in the name of the Lord and not in the name of *me*, my
attitude changes immediately. So next time you need to
make an adjustment based on circumstance ...be patient.
Seek God, and do whatever needs to be done in the name
of the Lord, and what you know to be right. *It is never
wrong to do the right thing!*

> And whatever you do, whether in word or deed, do it
> all in the name of the Lord Jesus, giving thanks to God
> the Father through him.
>
> Colossians 3:17

Once the adjustment has been made, you will get used to it and incorporate the change when making your next decision. Sometimes things just have to change to avoid calamity, and sometimes you see things, good things, when pursuing a new route.

He who guards his mouth and his tongue keeps himself from calamity.

Proverbs 21:23

There are lots of different ways or routes for us to follow in life. Beware of the warning signs!

And having been warned in a dream not to go back to Herod, they returned to their country by another route.

Matthew 2:12

Dear Lord, thank you for helping me to recognize adjustments that would serve to make my life filled with your riches. When I am weak and fearful and have no clue of how to make things different, remind me to *ask* for your wisdom, and then remind me to *trust you* and *your timing!* And God, I might need to be reminded often. I tend to easily lose focus. Amen.

Praise God wherever you are and whatever situation he has allowed you to be in. His glory will shine through!

wobbling
-october 6, 2006

"It's hard to stand on your own two feet when you don't even know your feet are back there." That was one of the first things Dr. Harris told me to be conscious of when Bentley started to regain use of the muscles in her legs. "Remind her that they are back there. Exercise them, pat them, massage them. Make her aware that there is a back part of her that is connected! It is important for her to stand as often as she can putting weight on those back legs while she eats, while she drinks, etc."

I laughed and thought, *Yeah really—get her to stand up and eat.* She has eaten on her belly since she we got her! Well, I have a strap that I put under her to hoist up her hind legs and we have put her food on a riser and there she *stands* (after getting help planting her feet) eating her food. I hold the strap loosely and as of the last few days, I haven't even had to use the strap. She needs a little help getting up and she tends to "list" a little but once she gets going she really stands on her own two feet.

Am I standing on my own two feet? Or am I having to be held up by the strap of shopping, or traveling, or food, or drinking, or gambling or relationships? When I get wobbly, what strap do I grab to steady my footing? There is only one sure fire way to stay steady! You and I can try different avenues all we want, but it comes back to ONLY one sure and steady reliable source for stability, and that is *God*. He is *unwavering!* He is *always* available! *He* is *consistent! He* is the *anchor* of any storm!

> He lifted me out of the slimy pit, out of the mud and mire; he set my feet on a rock and gave me a firm place to stand.
>
> Psalm 40:2

Once you see that you can stand on steady ground, you have the confidence to try it again and again. Pretty soon instead of the visible straps of restraint, you have the strap of *faith*. You can't see it, but you know it is there! Though the tangible straps appear to be of help, the help is only temporary. If used for a great amount of time they become a crutch for insecurity instead of a tool to help provide strength.

> …because it is by faith you stand firm.
>
> 2 Corinthians 1:24

> Therefore, my dear brothers, stand firm. Let nothing move you. Always give yourselves fully to the work of the LORD, because you know that your labor in the LORD is not in vain.
>
> 1 Corinthians 15:58

My dad is in his late eighties and he gets around just fine, but every once in a while he gets off balance just like all of us do. In my *mothering mode*, I'll say, "Dad, maybe it would help if you had a cane to give you support to help you get up out of a chair or walk on uneven concrete, etc."

His reply is always the same. "If I start that, I would get dependent on it, and I'm just fine right now!"

He's right and he is stronger for it. He is using those muscles and keeping them as strong as they can be. We have to use what we've got to keep it strengthened. Well, we've got *God*, and he will continue to strengthen us if we don't choose to use something else as a crutch in *his* place.

> But he who stands firm to the end will be saved.
>
> Matthew 24:13

> He makes my feet like the feet of a deer; he enables me to stand on the heights.
>
> Psalm 18:33

Everyday Bentley gets stronger, but it isn't easy for her. Getting strong in the *Lord* is not easy for any of us either; it takes time, discipline, repetition, and a willingness to adhere to a regime of prayer. For through prayer we are able to stand on our own two feet knowing that *God* is the muscle behind the strength, and *faith* is the strap that keeps us from wobbling!

> Now faith is being sure of what we hope for and certain
> of what we do not see.
>
> Hebrews 11:1

Dear Lord, I wobble all the time. Teach me to stand firm on my own two feet, knowing that you are the *muscle* within that keeps me strong, and it is my *faith* in *you* that keeps me on a steady path.

Praise God wherever you are and whatever situation he has allowed you to be in. His glory will shine through!

lab lessons
-october 8, 2006

Bentley is now nine-months-old, and Khaki, well she is the seasoned dog, the fifteen-year-old. Khaki has been around a long while and because she is older, she is considered wiser among her *one* peer. When I ask, "Do you want to go for a walk?" Bentley looks to Khaki to see how she is going to respond before showing any emotion …same *M.O.* when someone comes to the door. Are they friend or foe? Khaki is the lead dog. If she gets excited, Bentley follows with the same emotion. Barking, same deal. I just keep hoping that Bentley sees Khaki wagging her tail and will follow suit when she is finally able. They are devoted friends. Bentley affectionately helps to clean Khaki's face and ears and truly considers it an honor for Khaki to be still and let her. When Khaki submits to playing mouth-to-mouth fencing, you can imagine the *joy*. As I watch Bentley, I can see that Khaki is her role model. She not only wants to be like her; she wants to please her; she submits to her and does as she does. Bentley adores Khaki and holds her in awe. She depends on her. She learns from her!

I can't help but ask, do I have that relationship with Christ? Am I willing to be submissive? Do I set out to please God? Before I attempt to respond (to any situation) do I look first to Christ to see how he responds and then follow suit? There is a vast gap when comparing these relationships, I know, but it is about who you choose to look up to, who you take your cues from! These two dogs are pretty tight. How *tight* am I with Christ? If I do favor His ways then I should allow God's peace to absorb my fears. Why do I get scared when I know *him* to be confident? Why am I anxious when he would be calm? Why am I angry when he would be understanding? Why am I bitter when he would be content? Looking toward Khaki is not something Bentley plans to do. It is innate. It is a natural reaction, something that she doesn't *have* to remember to do.

> Those who look to him are radiant; their faces are never covered with shame.
>
> Psalm 34:5

> Look to the LORD and his strength; seek his face always.
>
> Psalm 105:4

I want to be like that. I want to behave naturally the way I should and not have to *think* about it, but it is impossible without the Lord's help. Oswald Chambers said in his October 7th devotional in *My Utmost for His Highest,* "It is revealed throughout the Bible that our Lord took on Himself the sin of the world through *identification with us,* not through *sympathy for us.*"[3] I have to be able to let

Christ reflect *his* identity in and through me because when I depend on just me, I am *off* the track a bunch more than I am *on* it. God's role is not to just understand me. He wants to transform me in a gradual way where I am no longer conscious of my behavior, but I just am doing and being according to the Christ who lives within me.

> Young men, in the same way be submissive to those who are older. All of you, clothe yourselves with humility toward one another, because, "God opposes the proud but gives grace to the humble."
>
> 1 Peter 5:5

> These are the men who divide you, who follow mere natural instincts and do not have the Spirit.
>
> Jude 1:19

Dear Lord, the next time I want to get out of sorts because of a situation that has hit me from behind, help me look first to you for a response and *then* react. Let me look to you in awe and with great respect. *Let me be dependent on you.* Let me be submissive to *your* way of "looking" at things, and let me affectionately "look" to you for cues and opportunities to share your light. Thank you for always staying close and for always being available!

Call to me and I will answer you and tell you great and unsearchable things you do not know.

Jeremiah 33:3

Thank you Lord for using the relationship of these two precious labs to show me lessons of dependence, friendship, respect, affection, and loyalty. For as Bentley keeps her eyes focused on Khaki, may I keep mine focused on you! Amen.

Praise God wherever you are and whatever situation he has allowed you to be in. His glory will shine through!

smelly, squeaky, toys
- october 12, 2006

My kids tell me that the dogs are color blind. I don't know how that piece of information has alluded me for so many years, but it has. Bentley has got some of the cutest toys in these wonderful colors (Khaki is too cool or maybe too old for toys), and I find out that dogs only see in black and white! So if not the colors then what's the pull? Why does Bentley like the ones that she likes and what makes certain ones her favorites? I've decided that the two draws are smell and noise. She has one *baby* that that she just sinks her nose in, doesn't hurt it, just wants it tucked in her front paws.

> If the whole body were an eye, where would the sense of hearing be? If the whole body were an ear, where would the sense of smell be?
>
> 1 Corinthians 12:17

How attracted are you to smells? This is one of my favorite senses: rain coming, gardenia plants, roses, something baking in the oven, freshly cut grass, an outdoor fire, soaps, perfumes, the smell of a clean baby with lotion etc. The thing about smells is that you know they are there, but you can't touch the smell. The only tangible way is to touch the object that the smell is attached to. Isn't that the way it is with God? You know he's there, but he is only tangible through the objects he has attached himself to: the Bible, people, nature, etc. God is tangible to us through *his* people and stories that reveal his example, his nature, his direction, and his love. As I see Bentley cuddle up with this rag a muffin toy, I too can see God willing to cuddle up with rag a muffin me. Not because I smell good but because he wants *me* to be a tangible object of *his* attraction. It is all about God; what he chooses, who he chooses, and how he orchestrates *his* plan. How *he* uses us, sometimes *we* will never know, but how *we* relate to *him*, it is *his* purpose to *know*. He constantly desires our attention and submission.

Another favorite of Bentley's is a barbell made out of squeaky tennis balls at either end. She can make this thing squeak in the fastest rhythmic motion. You think someone has got to be playing with her, but no, she has got the method down herself! Happy to be making noise for no apparent reason except she can!

Sometimes isn't that the way we are with our schedules? We are just squeaking along, making noises in a fast rhythmic motion and content with the rapid pace and the distractions of the world. If we had to *stop* and be quiet, we might have to reevaluate our priorities! Yikes! And that would cause us to step out of a comfortable familiar routine. Think about the last time, the TV was off, the music was off, there was no one around, and you were just still in the quietness of your own soul. Bet it's been a while! Maybe silence is what God longs for you to fight for so that he can bring thoughts of himself to your heart and mind. Instead of squeaking through life and just trying to *get through* one more day, *be still,* just for a few minutes, and realize the peace that there is in silence.

Be still, and know that I am God.

Psalm 46:10

The quiet words of the wise are more to be heeded than the shouts of a ruler of fools.

Ecclesiastes 9:17

Dear Lord, Help me to realize that I am an object of your attachment. Fill my heart with your love and my mind with your wisdom, and use my body for your glory. Help me not to fear silence but rather relish in the moments that you carve out to *be still* and know that you are God. Thank you for the sense of smell, of knowing the existence of something even though I can't touch it. Thank you that even though I can't touch you, you have made your presence known. O Lord, bless those who are wondering if you are real with a touch or a word or a glimpse of your mighty way. Let their eyes be opened to see the marvelous things you have done and look forward with hope of things to come. And, Lord, being *quiet* is something I have to fight for, so arm me for battle so I will be available to hear your whispers. Amen.

Praise God wherever you are and whatever situation he has allowed you to be in. His glory will shine through!

Part VI

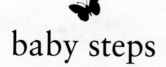

baby steps

Well, here we are in October, just over a month and a half after the accident. We are just moving along …one day at a time. We see a little progress but it is slow.

But still when I look at Bentley's sweet smile and her loving disposition, I can't help but be grateful that we made the choice that we did. I don't know what the future of her physical capabilities, only God does. But I an not in a position to do anything else but stay the path and keep praying and hoping that one day Bentley will again be able to be independent.

progress
-october 23, 2006

Bentley had a doctor's appointments all day on Tuesday. Her progress has been wonderful, and she again stands in the high percentile of animals responding after having this kind of spinal cord damage. Seldom has this much improvement been seen this early let alone improvement at all! God is forever faithful! These next three weeks will be the tell tale sign of whether she will be able to co-ordinate her standing and roll into a stride. My thought is *yes* she will!

Our last appointments were about a month ago, and we have stayed pretty close to schedule on what we were to do for exercises, herbs, etc. Yesterday, after examining her, the doctors felt that she is able to do much more that she is doing. But because she has had so much assistance, her mind says, just relax, take the help, don't push.

Things will be changing around here, and Bentley will be required to *carry* her weight much more often. She has progressed and will continue to do so, but as hard as it is, I have to back off! She has to be the one to work those muscles. She has to be motivated to stretch toward her capabilities. Instead of helping her progress, I will be holding her back if I continue to enable her to depend solely on cart help or strap lift. What we have done so far has been necessary, but now it is time *let go* and *let her* grow stronger.

Do I *carry* my weight? Do I allow God to push me in areas of discomfort, even if discomfort means backing off and letting go of control? Or am I content with the status quo? If I know something or someone is awry in my life, am I willing to address it or do I say, "Why bother?" or "It isn't worth it," or "What difference is it going to make?" or "It is too much trouble," or "Maybe later," or "It won't hurt if …"? Now is the time God has called us to make right something that is wrong. Yes, it might be hard, yes, it will be worth it, yes, it will make a difference, yes, it is worth bothering with, and yes, sometimes it is time to pull back.

Often times, God gives us this twinge of restlessness to make us aware that there is something or someone that he wants us to address. It is not fun when you feel that! It makes you uneasy, resentful, resistant, reluctant, and preoccupies your mind with thoughts that are dragging you down. Get it over with! Stretch. You've got it in you! I've got it in me! It comes down to are you and I willing to work? Ask God to guide your words and your ways. Don't try to conquer this battle alone. Don't. If you will let God be the guide, you will come out the victor each time. It might not look like it at that moment, but you will be on the high road. God will honor your obedience and faithfulness and most of all you will have exchanged a bag of worries for a paradise of peace. It doesn't matter how that someone else responds, what matters is how *you* did! *Carry* your weight to God, then let him help you work through the rest!

And anyone who does not carry his cross and follow me cannot be my disciple.

Luke 14:27

For each one should carry his own load.

Galatians 6:5

Being confident of this, that he who began a good work in you will carry it on to completion 'til the day of Christ Jesus.

Philippians 1:6

This is how we know that we love the children of God: by loving God and carrying out his commands.

1 John 5:2

Dear Lord, as I sit here typing these thoughts that run through my mind, I ask that you continue to guide me. Place upon my heart those things or people who I need to address even if it's only to pray for them. You alone know my thoughts and understand my concerns. Let me turn that bag of worries into a paradise of peace by obeying you as you gently nudge my heart to respond. Let me be motivated by your love which has been poured out in my heart by the Holy Spirit. Let me not cling on to the things of this world but attach myself to *you*. I am grateful, so grateful that you, the creator of this universe have such a personal interest in molding *me* in *your* likeness. May I be willing to submit to your ways. I know, Lord, that I fall back often, but there has been progress in my life as I look back, and I know you will not stop 'til you complete a good work within me. Amen

Praise God wherever you are or whatever situation he has allowed you to be in. His glory will shine through!

support
-october 24, 2006

Bentley is continuing to have good reports, even taking a few little baby steps. When she has to go outside, I use a strap beneath her back legs to help her with support. This helps keep her back feet from getting scraped on the cement. This has worked pretty well from the beginning, but she continues to grow and get stronger. Now she wants to go one way, and I want her to go another. Because I am behind her, I can't lead her, and she scrambles with all her might to go in the direction she pleases. Without a clear leader in sight, she is confused as to what direction she is to go …and she restlessly wanders having no clear guidance or direction in front of her. Then she hears, "Go get in your bed," and she heads toward the door. It works because this is a command she knows and she doesn't need a leader to carry it out, only a will!

If God has in fact offered to help us navigate through life, how do we respond? Do we, with all our strength, pull in the direction we want to go or do we wait to be led in God's direction. Is God behind you or in front of you? That is really the question? I so often times know what it is I am suppose to do or how I am suppose to respond my strength takes over and I pull with all my might to go in the direction I want with no regard as to the lead that I have been offered by God. Do I willfully contend to do the right thing?

Teach me to do your will, for you are my God; may your good Spirit lead me on level ground.

Psalm 143:10

Since you are my rock and my fortress, for the sake of your name lead and guide me.

Psalm 31:3

When Bentley and I are traveling with the same intention, it is so much easier to help her because she is willing to accept the help. I know there have been countless times when I have said, "God, I can do this myself," and I have fallen into frustration scraping my feet on the hard coinsequences along the way. "Where there is a will there is a way." We've been told all our lives! As I've gotten older I have found that to be so true. For if you submit *your* will to God's way things do work out for the best.

I will lead the blind by ways they have not known, along unfamiliar paths I will guide them; I will turn the darkness into light before them and make the rough places smooth. These are the things I will do; I will not forsake them."

Isaiah 42:16

Not that I have already obtained all this, or have already been made perfect, but I press on to take hold of that for which Christ Jesus took hold of me. Brothers, I do not consider myself yet to have taken hold of it. But one thing I do: Forgetting what is behind and straining toward what is ahead, I press on toward the goal to win the prize for which God has called me heavenward in Christ Jesus.

Philippians 3:12–14

And we know that in all things God works for the good of those who love him, who have been called according to his purpose.

Romans 8:28

Do not conform any longer to the pattern of this world, but be transformed by the renewing of your mind. Then you will be able to test and approve what God's will is—his good, pleasing, and perfect will.

Romans 12:2

Dear God, love me, teach me, forgive me, and guide me. Help me to know you and to follow your ways. Help me to accept your help with graciousness and appreciation. Remind me that it is not through my strength but yours that I am able to do all things that will bring about glory to your name. Lord, when I am straddling that strap of strength, remind me that it is in my best interest to be paralleled in purpose and direction with you. For if my life is to be transformed, I must trust your ways and lay mine aside. Amen.

Praise God wherever you are and whatever situation he has allowed you to be in. His glory will shine through!

baby steps
-october 27, 2006

"Shocking, just shocking," the physical therapist at the vet said when she saw Bentley. She could not believe what has transpired over the last week. Bentley is walking like a baby, a little wobbly, but picking up her feet one foot in front of the other and moving forward a few steps at a time. I knew God loved five percent odds. I worked with Bentley after they told me last week she was much more capable than she was letting on. I walked behind her picking up her back feet for her one by one and showing her *how* to walk. She picked it up quickly and has improved each day—today more than ever!

> If the LORD delights in a man's way, he makes his steps firm.
>
> Psalm 37:23

(I hope the above verse rolls over to a man's *dog* too.)

> I have considered my ways and have turned my steps to your statutes.
>
> Psalm 119:59

Since we live by the Spirit, let us keep in step with the
Spirit.

Galatians 5:25

What about me? Am I more capable that I am letting
on, able to take baby steps and move forward but just not
doing it? Do I need a little push or encouragement or a
"how to" lesson? Sometimes baby steps are the only way
to get started when you are trying something new. God is
right there behind you helping you put one foot in front
of the other, and then when he feels like you are catching
on, he moves to the front and entices you with *his* lead. I
used treats for Bentley. What is God enticing you with?
If it has something to do with helping others people,
listen carefully, no matter how *out there* it may seem, for
God is in the business of shaping people. His concern
is for *his* children and their souls. He will do whatever
it takes to get their attention, and you might be the one
he has chosen for *his* job or you just might be the job of
His hand!

My sheep listen to my voice; I know them, and they
follow me.

John 10:27

Do not merely listen to the word, and so deceive
yourselves. Do what it says.

James 1:22

Bentley only had a five percent chance to ever walk again. Out of town vets had given up on her at the very beginning because she felt no "deep pain," and it was advised that we put her down. Just remember that no matter how slim the odds are God will not give up on you or the struggle you are enduring. Have faith, take the little steps, and see how God will encourage you and hang with you along the way. It takes courage to start something new, sometimes even to continue something old, and even if you feel a little wobbly, God will give you his strength to persevere through any trial! Be it people or circumstance!

Not only so, but we also rejoice in our sufferings, because we know that suffering produces perseverance.

Romans 5:3

Therefore, since we are surrounded by such a great cloud of witnesses, let us throw off everything that hinders and the sin that so easily entangles, and let us run with perseverance the race marked out for us.

Hebrews 12:1

(Just a note here on this verse. The word entangle. Think of fish being caught in a net, how they are flopping around, trapped, wanting so greatly to be free. Sin does that to us)

Consider it pure joy, my brothers, whenever you face trials of many kinds, because you know that the testing of your faith develops perseverance. Perseverance must finish its work so that you may be mature and complete, not lacking anything.

James 1:3–4

The above verse is one of my favorite verses …just consider …it joy? Hard to do when things are pretty unstable around you …but we can have a true and confident joy in knowing that God is above all things and in all situations. His authority is above all others, and through God's grace we are able to rely on what we believe instead of what it is we see.

Dear Lord, teach me to walk with you step by step and when things get hard remind me to hang in there because you are hanging in there with me. Even if I am wobbly, at least I am moving and trying. Teach me to persevere in spite of the outlook, for one thing we know is there is *always* hope, and through it all, our character will develop through the faith in God that we practice. I love you, Lord and am so very grateful today as everyday for your involvement in my life. Release me from the entanglements that I allow myself to get trapped in, and teach me step by step to avoid the nets of sin that entrap me. Amen.

There is a Christian song, "Sometimes by Step" sung by Rich Mullins whose chorus is:

> Oh God, You are my God
> And I will ever praise You
> Oh God, You are my God
> And I will ever praise You
> I will seek You in the morning
> And I will learn to walk in Your way
> And step by step You'll lead me
> And I will follow You all of my days[4]

I can't get it out of my head.

Praise God wherever you are and whatever situation he has allowed you to be in. His glory will shine through!

perception
-november 1, 2006

Bentley and Khaki were fencing with their mouths on the kitchen floor while my grandson Blake was watching. He watched with such emotion, and, finally, you could just tell by the grimace on his face and his quivering lip that he was going to start crying hard. It was the perception he had. The dogs are generally quiet, sniffing around, giving kisses, or just laying around watching him. This was new, and it looked mean. They were making growling, guttural noises, and it was fast dueling with all teeth showing. How could he know that *this* was pure affection and entertainment to each of them? His little imagination and concept of the world are so limited.

We think that because we have been around the block a few times and aren't watching our first "rodeo" that we have a handle on perspectives, and we just don't. Our imaginations are just not grand enough to conceive the precepts of our Holy God, and our concept, well, instead of being perceived through God's intellect, it only passes through ours. Something that is familiar. We deal with trials and potholes that have been allowed in our lives thinking, *What did I do to deserve this?* And the real answer is nothing! It is by God's grace that we have been given challenges. (Choices and consequences of those choices are a different matter!) I know that seems to be a distorted way of looking at it, but consider, God pursues the weak instead of the strong, the dependent instead of the independent, the poor instead of the rich, the brokenhearted instead of the prideful so why wouldn't his concept of trials be *good* instead of *bad*. It is!

But God chose the foolish things of the world to shame the wise; God chose the weak things of the world to shame the strong.

1 Corinthians 1:27

Listen, my dear brothers: Has not God chosen those who are poor in the eyes of the world to be rich in faith and to inherit the kingdom he promised those who love him?

James 2:5

The LORD is close to the brokenhearted and saves those who are crushed in spirit.

Psalm 34:18

Pride only breeds quarrels, but wisdom is found in those who take advice.

Proverbs 13:10

The end of a matter is better than its beginning, and patience is better than pride.

Ecclesiastes 7:8

The eyes of the arrogant man will be humbled and the pride of men brought low; the LORD alone will be exalted in that day.

Isaiah 2:11

Blessed are the poor in spirit, for theirs is the kingdom of heaven.

Matthew 5:3

We are so lazy in our motivations to be more mature, to grow, to deepen our convictions, to be selfless instead of selfish because it stretches parts of us that we don't want to exercise. (I hate that word. I am convicted each time, and I so need to be doing that.) God is in the business of stretching because stretching causes each of us to be a little more flexible and pliable, and when we are pliable, we are easier to mold. We can just go on day by day in the comfort zone of choice, or we can make a conscious decision to change our perspective on trials and potholes and look to see where and how God is going to use them to *make us better!*

Remember that you molded me like clay. Will you now turn me to dust again?

Job 10:9

My comfort in my suffering is this: Your promise preserves my life.

Psalm 119:50

Shout for joy, O heavens; rejoice, O earth; burst into
song, O mountains! For the LORD comforts his people
and will have compassion on his afflicted ones.

Isaiah 49:13

When you feel like the insides of you are wrestling back
and forth that is a good thing because it means God
is in there stirring up a part of you that has remained
comfortable and tucked away in a dark corner of oblivion
within you. Don't look at adversity as the world sees it,
not just in yourself but in others and what is happening
in their lives, but ask God to let you see it through *his*
perspective; for his concept of change is always for our
betterment and good not for calamity and unrest.

How long must I wrestle with my thoughts and every
day have sorrow in my heart? How long will my enemy
triumph over me?"

Psalm 13:2

God did not promise a life of comfort but rather a comfort
of peace as we live life.

Dear Lord, Thank you for the trials you send and
for the wrestling within my soul. For those are the very
emotions that remind me that you love me so much that
you would allow my pain for your gain. My imagination
is limited, Lord, so limited, but you have the capacity

to let me see glimpses of your workings not only in my life but in the lives of those I love. Remind me that the *hard* way is sometimes the *best* way and it is through the deepest darkest times in my life that you show yourself so vividly. Bless my friends O Lord, and my family. May you touch each of them with the comfort of your peace as they face, head on, the challenges that have been allowed in their lives. You are a gracious God, filled with love and compassion. Blessed are we to know you and be invited to be in your countenance. Amen.

Praise God wherever you are and whatever situation he has allowed you to be in. His glory will shine through!

hansel and gretel
-november 3, 2006

Remember Hansel and Gretel. To keep from getting lost in the woods, they dropped breadcrumbs to mark their way. I thought about this story this week as I was in the front yard trying to entice Bentley to practice walking. I started with a treat, breaking it in half, and realized this is going to make her to heavy to lift herself with all the treats I would have to use, so I pulled out the Cheerios and dropped them on the ground one by one. Bentley walked slowly all the way around the yard examining and following the path of Cheerios, picking up one at a time. When she completed the round, she had no idea the workout she had just accomplished. She had concentrated on the little things and the exercise was a non-issue, but oh, she unknowingly received great benefit through the process.

For a man's ways are in full view of the LORD, and he examines all his paths.

Proverbs 5:21

Let us examine our ways and test them, and let us return to the LORD.

Lamentations 3:40

Examine yourselves to see whether you are in the faith;
test yourselves. Do you not realize that Christ Jesus is in
you—unless, of course, you fail the test?

2 Corinthians 13:5

What has been scattered along your path to keep you
moving. I think God too gives us a few of *his* crumbs
to examine and nibble on as we walk, sometimes it is
something someone has said, something you read, maybe
a picture that caught your eye or even a kind gesture.

Often times we forget the walking part because we are
so focused on the crumbs and one day we wake up and
realize I made it through the storm! The whole picture is
just sometimes too much to look at. We probably would
do better to approach life taking in a little at a time. It
will work out! The older that I get I realize "things do
work out" but we have to be patient and not forfeit the
little ordinary pieces of life that make up the *big picture.
For God does not call the extraordinary to do ordinary things
but he calls the ordinary to do extraordinary things.* It is in
the small insignificant moments that reflect the glory of
our awesome God. Oswald Chambers says in his Oct 25
devotional from My Utmost for His Highest book, "All
of God's people are ordinary people who have been made
extraordinary by the purpose he has given them."[5]

What is the purpose he has given you? It might be
so ordinary that you don't even realize it *is* the purpose.
God takes the little things and makes them grand in his
kingdom. You are making a contribution!

The LORD will fulfill his purpose for me; your love, O
LORD, endures forever—do not abandon the works of
your hands.

Psalm 138:8

For our light and momentary troubles are achieving for
us an eternal glory that far outweighs them all.

2 Corinthians 4:17

The difference in Hansel and Gretel is that their crumbs
lead to the witch's house, the crumbs God sends will lead
us straight to *his heart*. There are a bunch of different uses
for Cheerios; eating, counting, cooking, but today when
I discovered that that were the perfect light snack and
enticement for Bentley, it was a such reminder that it is
the *little*, ordinary things that God uses to shake up our
thoughts and encourage our walk (with him). Cheerios,
you can't get much more ordinary than that! Just think of
how many uses God can find in us to bring glory to his
name.

When they saw the courage of Peter and John and
realized that they were unschooled, ordinary men, they
were astonished and they took note that these men had
been with Jesus.

Acts 4:13

Dear Lord, thank you for the ordinary moments of life. Help me to be directed through your Holy Spirit to the purpose that you have for my life. Remind me that what seems to be insignificant crumbs that you scatter are just what you have intended as encouragement as I walk with you. Lead me to the path that you desire and then Lord will you please walk with me down the road the whole way. I need you as my constant companion. For the visits, the wisdom, the way, the tender friendship and your shelter. Amen.

Praise God wherever you are and whatever situation he has allowed you to be in. His glory will shine through!

pattern
-november 7, 2006

Do not conform any longer to the pattern of this world, but be transformed by the renewing of your mind. Then you will be able to test and approve what God's will is—his good, pleasing and perfect will.

Romans 12:2

This verse has taken hold of my thoughts. I was thinking about Bentley and how we have changed her morning "pattern." This must confuse her to change a pattern. "What is the difference between a pattern and a habit?" As I tried to think through that without a dictionary this verse just kept popping up, kind of like those pop-ups on the computer. It just wouldn't go away. "Pattern" of the world. Why didn't they say "habit" of the world? Stop here a minute and think …how would you describe pattern vs. habit? This is what I came up with: a pattern is a form that you follow, a habit is something that you do over and over again. To follow a pattern is a conscious choice of conformation. Following a habit is in an unconscious awareness of redoing the same thing. You don't think, *I am going to brush my teeth.* it is just something that you do because you have done it over and over for so long. Back to this verse:

Do not: stop.

Conform: trying to be just like something or someone you see.

Any Longer: change your action.

To the pattern of this world: and don't let the world be a magnate and pull you into behavior which contradicts the way God has shown us to live.

But be transformed: remember those transformer figures that were so popular many years back—you could change them into something completely different than their original appearance.

By the renewing of your mind: incorporate something or someone "new" in your thoughts; allow God to refresh your mind.

Then: this is a big word because you first have to do something before the next thing will happen.

You will be able: you then are releasing your mind from captivity of old ways and openly have allowed thoughts of a good and better approach to life.

To test and approve what God's will is: and you will be able to peacefully weigh good from bad and even good from best.

His good and perfect and pleasing will: so that you will know what it is that God has planned for this precious life of yours that he created.

A Pattern is a combination of qualities or acts or tendencies that forms a consistent arrangement whereas *a habit is* an acquired behavior pattern regularly followed.

If a pattern is followed 'til it turns into a habit then maybe God is saying don't conform to the patterns of this world because after exposure over and over the world's standards will become our unconscious values.

Just look at what has become "lukewarm" as far as values, morality, violence, and apathy through television. I often times tend to accept what is fed to me through media and don't take time or initiative to measure the input according to God's standards. What patterns are you and I following? How are the world's standards influencing our decisions, our relationships, our perceptions, and our behavior?

Dear Lord, I *have* conformed to the standards of this world in so many ways. Please open my eyes, ears and mind to *think* rather than just *accept* what is sent my way. Let me have courage to stand up when the views are contradictory to what I know is to be truth and a Godly way of living. Convict me when I am lukewarm, and, Lord, remind me that you have sent me a pattern of how to live through your word and your example when you were here on this Earth. It adheres to your good and perfect and pleasing will. Let me be content to abide within your boundaries and not be suckered into chasing the follies of this world. Amen.

Praise God wherever you are and whatever situation he has allowed you to be in. His glory will shine through!

old dog
-november 8, 2006

Who said you can't teach old dogs new tricks? Bentley and Khaki were in the kitchen. My son Tom was trying to teach Bentley to catch with a tennis ball. For days this has gone on, and tonight when I threw the ball to Bentley and she missed it, Khaki, for the first time jumped up and retrieved it. So I tossed it to Khaki, who hasn't seemed to want anything to do with play, and she caught it. I thought, *This must be a fluke,* so I threw it again and she caught it again. This went on for several minutes. I was amazed. Bentley was annoyed.

All this time, Khaki had been ignored when we played because I didn't think she was interested and didn't think she was even able to play, but the deal is I never gave her a chance! I didn't ask her or invite her to play. (This was a game Tom and Mel played with her when she was younger. I had forgotten.)

We are often so busy making decisions for those that we love that I think sometimes we don't give them a chance to *play* and use their skills. For they often sit quietly watching, and as my mom would say, "they follow the line of least resistance because they can . " Maybe it isn't only those we love maybe it is *us.* Are you possibly one of the ones sitting on the sidelines hesitant to engage in play? Waiting for someone to encourage you to *get up* and *get going!*

> Sing to him a new song; play skillfully, and shout for
> joy.
>
> Psalm 33:3

I think of the times that I sit pondering instead of doing; I wonder if I could run a marathon? Own my own company? Speak at a conference? Make a hole in one? Rehabilitate a paralyzed dog? Not eat chocolate for a week? How will I ever know unless I am willing to get off the sidelines and *try!* That little voice that says, *Don't even try. It isn't worth the time or effort* is a sissy. (I love that word.) *If* it is something that has captivated your thoughts and you feel like it measures up to a good and pleasing will of God, then what are you waiting for? What am I waiting for?

> Test me, O LORD, and try me, examine my heart and my mind.
>
> Psalm 26:2

> "Sir," the invalid replied, "I have no one to help me into the pool when the water is stirred. While I am trying to get in, someone else goes down ahead of me."
>
> John 5:7

Just imagine sitting on the ground and someone walks up, extends you a hand to help you get up, and says come on. What are you going to do? Do you take the hand for help? Or say I can do it myself? The hand is God's. Let him help you up and start standing, then stretch towards your goal or your dream. You can do it with God's helping hand.

> Are you so foolish? After beginning with the Spirit, are you now trying to attain your goal by human effort?
>
> Galatians 3:3

Dear Lord, Thank you for the reminder that often times there are qualified participants sitting on the sidelines who haven't been encouraged to engage in life's joyful endeavors. Help me to stand *back* when I need to let another stand *up* and play and use the skills that you have given them. And when it is time for me to stand, help me up and give me courage to try something new. Amen.

Praise God wherever you are and whatever situation he has allowed you to be in. His glory will shine through.

moving on

Bentley is gaining momentum at a snail's pace,; now we are just trying to figure out what accessories we need to protect her hind legs and help her with her stability. When she is up, and trying to walk, her hind leg muscles are not strong enough to lift each foot for each step, so she ends up dragging them. And that is like having a nail file on nails that are already too short. We are looking at aids to help her and, believe it or not, there is a lot out there to chose from. We will start with shoes for her feet, but we also need to figure out how to protect her legs when she wants to go fast and starts dragging her body. Each phase of recovery brings on new challenges

get a grip
-november 9, 2006

Bentley got some new tennis shoes this week, thick rubber soled tennis shoes for dogs. Okay, maybe you think I have lost it, but you can't imagine how much they have helped. Her hind leg muscles are weak, and gripping the ground to get a solid stand is tough, not to mention that the concrete is tearing at her paws when she tries to dart from the grass. Now, in the morning before I take her out, we have to put her shoes on. I think she likes them or at least likes the stability they have afforded her.

Remember the phrase "get a grip." It is one of those sayings that has lost its steam after a few years, but it was an ever so prevalent term in my house for a while. Life shoves us a bunch of slippery, can't get your arms around situations, and sometimes it is hard to "get a grip," and we need some *rubber meets the road* wisdom. Oh, we've got the how to books and the friendly free advise stuff, but where is the real truth and who is the one that really has our best interest in mind for no other reason than love, for the sake of loving us.

For God so loved the world that he gave his one and only Son, that whoever believes in him shall not perish but have eternal life.

John 3:16

No, the Father himself loves you because you have loved
me and have believed that I came from God.

John 16:27

God is there, right beside you when the world is twirling
and there seems to be no way out. He IS the rubber that
meets the road he is the one who can help you get a grip
and stand solid even when the winds around you are
throwing you off balance.

He lifted me out of the slimy pit, out of the mud and
mire; he set my feet on a rock and gave me a firm place
to stand.

Psalm 40:2

I have a saying in my house that says, "Sometimes God
calms the storm and sometimes God lets the storm rage
and calms the child."

When the storm has swept by, the wicked are gone, but
the righteous stand firm forever.

Proverbs 10:25

It is all about solid footing. Maybe you are in a storm
now or maybe one is just around the corner getting ready

to blow your way. Maybe one has just blown through and left unsettling remnants for you to deal with. Get ready, put your shoes on and be able to stand solid and stand firm. Our God is a God of steel, which you can lean on with confidence and trust. He will not crater. He is strong, mighty, and steady and is a beacon to adhere to as we are tossed through life's uncertainties. For us to get a grip on life we have to be willing to submit to the strength, the wisdom and the might of God who has been deemed worthy. He has proven his ability to accomplish the possible in what we have declared impossible.

> Nevertheless, God's solid foundation stands firm, sealed with this inscription: "The LORD knows those who are his," and, "Everyone who confesses the name of the LORD must turn away from wickedness.
>
> 2 Timothy 2:19

> For nothing is impossible with God.
>
> Luke 1:37

Be steady in the love of God. Be steady in his truth. Be steady in the confidence of knowing he is beside you in any situation. Be steady in knowing there is nothing you have done that God will not forgive if you ask him to. Be steady in accepting the fact that life is hard when you go at it alone. We all need help, and God's help is ever present at all times.

When you need to "get a grip", there is nothing so gripping as a relationship with the Lord Jesus Christ. He is available, but are you, am I?

Dear Lord, You are the steady rock on which we can stand firm. When the winds of unrest swirl through our hearts, calm us with your peace, and comfort us with your presence. When we lose our grip, grip us and keep us from falling. You are a God that proves the impossible is possible. Help us to trust that though things may seem dreary for while your heavenly hand will declare victory for all of your children! Amen

Praise God wherever you are and whatever situation he has allowed you to be in. His glory will shine through!

swimming
- november 10, 2006

As I was watching Bentley swim today, I focused on the movement of her hind legs. She was kicking with ease and confidence as she fetched her ball. Her buoyancy allowed her to move with greater ease and confidence. She isn't stumbling because her paws are stepping lightly when she skims the steps.

When we are immersed in faith, trusting, and knowing God and the power behind his plans, we are able to step a little lighter too. We are not emerged in worry and steeped with stress because the focus is on our faith and not the problem. When Bentley is out of the water, she unconsciously has to focus on on each step ... with a deliberate intention of walking to her intended spot (except when there is food around ...and then she slides in on her rear with great speed). When she is swimming, body weight is not an issue, because she is being held up by the water that surrounds her. Same with us. When we are not tuned into God and our faith in him is on the back burner, we seem to focus on the weight of ourselves and our problems. When we are truly centered and surrounded by faith and trusting God, the issues lose their momentum and we are lightened by an internal hope.

To you, O Lord, I lift up my soul.

Psalm 25:1

Humble yourselves before the Lord, and he will lift you up.

James 4:10

Humble yourselves, therefore, under God's mighty hand, that he may lift you up in due time.

1 Peter 5:6

Next time you wash you hands and see that water running through your fingers, think about letting God carry your burdens. Lighten your load and immerse yourself in the power, the protection, the wisdom, and the truth that God has offered.

"When you pass through the waters, I will be with you; and when you pass through the rivers, they will not sweep over you. When you walk through the fire, you will not be burned; the flames will not set you ablaze."

Isaiah 43:2

Dear Lord, Let me be immersed in faith and bring to you the troubles of my day. Lighten my load by lifting my focus on me and transferring that focus to you. Give me the freedom to live *light* instead of carrying unnecessary burdens. I know that when I try to walk on *my* solid ground, I fumble and get frustrated with my efforts. Forgive me for not responding to you when you have been so kind to offer yourself as a help and a guide. I want to be able to float through the hard stuff, and I know that I can only achieve that freedom through a personal relationship with you not just once in a while but everyday! Amen.

Praise God wherever you are and whatever situation he has allowed you to be in. His glory will shine through!

sacrifice

-november 14, 2006

Everyday we are called to make sacrifices. We were out of town this weekend and Tom and Molly were the designated dog sitters. Ordinarily, a dog sitter is a blow off job, but in the case of Bentley, it does have its challenges. Early wake up calls, a few messes along the way, she needs a little help getting outside, etc. But they were willing to sacrifice their time and schedules to accommodate our needs for a sitter and Bentley's need for a caretaker. There was a reward, and this brings up a good point.

Do we sacrifice only when we know there will be a reward or do we sacrifice without expectation knowing it is what God would have us do? As for Tom and Molly, they would have offered to sit anyway but the reward sure made it sweeter. Sacrifice is giving up something of importance to ourselves on behalf of something important to someone else. It is the ability to let go of a stronghold of selfish pursuit and put someone else's needs in front of our own.

We do that for our children, our parents, our friends etc. But are we willing and have we made ourselves available to sacrifice for God? Are we willing to sacrifice control, sacrifice embarrassment, sacrifice pride, sacrifice strategy, sacrifice pleasure, sacrifice comfort, and in Abraham's instance, sacrifice a child? I am not sure I am so willing, and I am not sure my faith is that strong. But I want it to be, and I strive for it to be.

When we sacrifice for God's purposes, most of the time, we don't know the answers to the why's or the how's or the when's that will result; for we are not to sacrifice conditionally only willingly. God has got it all worked out; we just need to let go of "our" way and be on the lookout for "God's" way, which most times involves loving others *more than* ourselves.

> Then God said, "Take your son, your only son, Isaac, whom you love, and go to the region of Moriah. Sacrifice him there as a burnt offering on one of the mountains I will tell you about.
>
> Genesis 22:2

God has called us to be in perfect union with his will. How can we be in perfect union if we don't know what his will is? And how can we know *what* his will is if we don't know *who* he is? And how can we know who he is unless we take the time to establish a relationship with him?

God was willing to sacrifice on our behalf his son, his only son! He sacrificed someone he loved and cherished, giving up someone of great importance to him on behalf of the greater importance to us. His reward to us was eternal life and forgiveness and freedom from the consequences of our sin.

Unlike the other high priests, he does not need to offer sacrifices day after day, first for his own sins, and then for the sins of the people. He sacrificed for their sins once for all when he offered himself.

Hebrews 7:27

He is the atoning sacrifice for our sins, and not only for ours but also for the sins of the whole world.

1 John 2:2

Don't you sometimes wonder how you could repay someone who has made a significant difference in your life? Maybe your parents, your spouse, your children, a dear friend? Well God is the someone who has made a significant difference in all of our lives, and the only reward we could possible bestow to/on him that would have any value is acceptance! Acceptance of the fact that his son is who he says he is, the acceptance of an invitation to join God as he pursues his plans, and the acceptance of sacrifice when it is called for to reflect his authority and our trust in *his* mighty ways.

[Living Sacrifices] "Therefore, I urge you, brothers, in view of God's mercy, to offer your bodies as living sacrifices, holy and pleasing to God—this is your spiritual act of worship."

Romans 12:1

And do not forget to do good and to share with others,
for with such sacrifices God is pleased.

Hebrews 13:16

Our God reigns; no matter what is going on in this crazy
world, he reigns. We are called to show his love that is in
us through the sacrifice we willingly and joyfully make to
one another.

This is love: not that we loved God, but that he loved us
and sent his Son as an atoning sacrifice for our sins.

1 John 4:10

Dear Lord, I am but an ordinary child in this world who
you have counted as one of your own. I am willing to
sacrifice what I have and who I am into your hands for
your glory. I will say that I am not always so "Johnny on
the spot" ready to sacrifice. Often times, you will find I
am reluctant to respond, because I don't know what the
outcome will be. I ask that you continue to fortify my
spirit with your love, your power, and your courage as I
learn day by day to trust you. No matter how scary the
sacrifice may be, I just keep thinking about Abraham!
I want to be as *faithful* as he was. I want to have such
assured trust in you that I am internally programmed to
respond to your call no matter what that call may be. (I

know you are working on that and I thank you.) And Lord, there are no words to Thank you for the sacrifice of your son, the loving atonement that you propitiated on our behalf. You have deemed us worthy of such a gift and may we in turn take this gift and offer it to the folks who you put in our path. Amen.

Praise God wherever you are and whatever situation he has allowed you to be in. His glory will shine through!

needs
-november 15, 2006

We all have needs. When I walked into the kitchen and saw the basket that holds the dog toys torn into shreds, I realized that one of Bentley's needs is to chew. If I don't supply her with a good chew bone then chances are she will find something else to fulfill her desire to chew, and she did!

What happens when our needs are not met? The thing about a dog is they can't talk. You learn a bunch from looking at their face, and knowing their habits but there is a certain amount of calculated guesswork. Some of it is just plain ole common sense. Some needs, if you are paying attention are right there in your face.

Consideration and imposition are two completely opposite ways to transpose our needs on others. And they usually have two completely opposite reactions. Last week I imposed one of my needs or wants on Mel. I added Bentley to Mel's "grab the paper routine with Khaki," not considering how much trouble Bentley is and that Mel is dressed for work, and is on a pretty routine schedule. Instead of being considerate of him, I was imposing when it wasn't at all necessary or even very helpful. I just thought it would be fun for Bentley, but she's a dog not one of our children. I realized after she made the simple morning outing of getting the paper a total pain in the neck that "I" had not been considerate of my husband's schedule and was looking at it only from my point of view (it would be fun)!

I think we all have a tendency to impose our thoughts, opinions, way to do things, and preferences on those around us without often times taking into consideration their needs. We all have needs. Some of us have more than others or at least think we do. It is courtesy to try to understand the different ways that you and someone else might respond to the same situation and not be so demanding that your way be the prevalent way.

> If it is encouraging, let him encourage; if it is contributing to the needs of others, let him give generously; if it is leadership, let him govern diligently; if it is showing mercy, let him do it cheerfully.
>
> Romans 12:8

> Do not let any unwholesome talk come out of your mouths, but only what is helpful for building others up according to their needs, that it may benefit those who listen.
>
> Ephesians 4:29

God is in the business of meeting out needs but often what we *think* we need and what God *knows* we need are very different. I have to be willing to ask God to give me what he knows is right and be satisfied with his response. So many times if I would just think and not hurry and

"do" so fast, I would be able to walk in someone else's'
shoes and not impose my ways and my style onto their
lives.

And my God will meet all your needs according to his
glorious riches in Christ Jesus.

Philippians 4:19

Do nothing out of selfish ambition or vain conceit, but
in humility consider others better than yourselves.

Philippians 2:3

But the wisdom that comes from heaven is first of all
pure; then peace-loving, considerate, submissive, full of
mercy and good fruit, impartial and sincere.

James 3:17

Husbands, in the same way be considerate as you live
with your wives, and treat them with respect as the
weaker partner and as heirs with you of the gracious
gift of life, so that nothing will hinder your prayers.

1 Peter 3:7

We all are doing the best we can. Or are we? Maybe we
should be striving for God's best in us and through us.
When we take time to listen to others, we should try
to understand where they are coming from and maybe
where they have been. Then we would be a little better

at recognizing their needs. I just think about how many times I put mine first. Consideration does take a little more time than imposition, but consideration is something we do for others and imposition is something we do from a selfish bent. God always considers us—and our needs—without imposing. He waits for an invitation from us for him to join us instead of pushing his way in and imposing his ways. God has designed an example for us to follow and tells us how we should treat others. The problem is: we often don't choose to put someone else's needs in front of our own.

He who forms the hearts of all, who considers everything they do

Psalm 33:15

And let us consider how we may spur one another on toward love and good deeds.

Hebrews 10:24

Dear Lord, You have created us as we are, with needs, preferences, opinions, and bents. We each are different and have needs that we don't even know how to fulfill, but you do. Let us be open to your persuasions and your offerings in our life. Let us be willing to put others first and try to understand what it is that makes them tick. Let us be able to look a little harder and a little longer before we make unfair judgments. Help us to choose to be available when we see a need and react to it the best we know how. Help us to be considerate of others and not impose our ways on others based on our own needs or wants. Make us mindful Lord of the undeserving consideration that you show to us each day. Amen.

Praise God wherever you are and whatever situation he has allowed you to be in. His glory will shine through!

training
-november 22, 2006

Bentley continues to improve. On her wheeled cart, we have transformed the two back stirrups, which have held her hind legs into one strap now supporting only her belly. She now is using her legs to walk where she used to only be able to drag them. If you saw her, you would think her walk resembled the strides of someone who has been over served. She is in training.

We too are in training. Spiritual training. God is the coach. He pushes us out of a comfort zone and through encouragement and support of chosen onlookers; he gives us the initiative to push toward a goal of his choosing. When we were created, God placed in us a void that only he could fill. No matter how much we succeeded or gathered or triumphed, we would still be looking for fulfillment. It is like a circle; the crave is never complete because you need something to break the cycle. Reminds me of those suitcases on the baggage claim belt. They just keep going around and around 'til someone finally claims them.

Train a child in the way he should go, and when he is old he will not turn from it.

Proverbs 22:6

A student is not above his teacher, but everyone who is fully trained will be like his teacher.

Luke 6:40

Everyone who competes in the games goes into strict training. They do it to get a crown that will not last; but we do it to get a crown that will last forever.

1 Corinthians 9:25

This week, I was watching the video of Jamie Ann's (my daughter) rehearsal dinner (from a year ago) and reflecting on a part of the toast that Mel gave. He said that marriage is a team sport, and you have to work together to achieve a successful end result. But if you listen and respect God as your coach, he'll teach you strategies of success. When you fumble he'll show you how to get right up and brush right off and get back in the game. He will show us how to work with what we have got now! Don't give up. Figure out what went wrong and try to avoid it for the next time. (Those were not exact quotes but you get the idea.)

God wants us to claim *him* as our friend and confidant and savior. He wants you to recognize that there is a void and ask him to fill it.

Not that we are competent in ourselves to claim anything for ourselves, but our competence comes from God.

2 Corinthians 3:5

When Bentley had her accident, there was a wreck on the spinal cord highway. She severely damaged the nerves leading from her brain to the nerves and muscles responding to the back half of her body. Everything just crashed. She has had to work hard to establish an alternate route of communication. Sometimes, I think there is a breakdown in our spiritual communication, and we have to reroute our thinking and change a few thoughts and perceptions to get the circuits going again. In order to shape up and reconnect we have to be willing to train!

The source of our training lies within us.

And, once made perfect, he became the source of eternal salvation for all who obey him.

Hebrews 5:9

Are we willing to submit to the coach who created us? Are we willing to let Christ exercise the fulfillment he has offered us through the void that He created? All of you reading these stories are a team, a mighty team, that God has called to work together for *his* glory. May we not just be doing for doing sake, and not just be speaking for speaking sake. May we be fulfilled with a purpose, no matter how insignificant we think it may be, knowing that God is working for *Goodness sake,* and he is using our team to make this world a better place. We all are working at different stations but one day the route will be connected.

No discipline seems pleasant at the time, but painful. Later on, however, it produces a harvest of righteousness and peace for those who have been trained by it.

Hebrews 12:11

His divine power has given us everything we need for life and godliness through our knowledge of him who called us by his own glory and goodness.

2 Peter 1:3

Dear Lord, thank you for creating a void within us, and thank you for the realization that no matter how much we do or how much we have or how much we contribute, we will always be left unsatisfied 'til we come to know you as a friend and a savior. May we be open to your coaching in our lives and may we strive to be disciplined in our training. No matter how hard the workout may be. Amen.

Praise God wherever you are and whatever situation he has allowed you to be in. His glory will shine through!

Part VIII

in need of wisdom

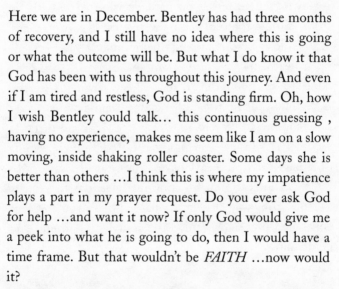

Here we are in December. Bentley has had three months of recovery, and I still have no idea where this is going or what the outcome will be. But what I do know it that God has been with us throughout this journey. And even if I am tired and restless, God is standing firm. Oh, how I wish Bentley could talk… this continuous guessing , having no experience, makes me seem like I am on a slow moving, inside shaking roller coaster. Some days she is better than others …I think this is where my impatience plays a part in my prayer request. Do you ever ask God for help …and want it now? If only God would give me a peek into what he is going to do, then I would have a time frame. But that wouldn't be *FAITH* …now would it?

And God is always working on a way to keep me faithful in who he is and what he is doing even if, or maybe especially if, I don't know how it will turn out!

From: Cathy
To: Prayer Warriors
Sent: December 6, 2006
Subject: Tough Decisions for Bentley

The following is not a devotional; it is just a window into how I come to the Lord with a specific need. When I find myself teetering on hard decisions, I humbly go to the throne room of God and request his wisdom and leadership. These comments below reflect my plea, my open heart, my lack of wisdom and my need for Lord's hand to be upon me. I send this knowing that you have followed the trials of our dog Bentley and we are now coming to crossroads where decisions are made as whether it is to keep on and wait for continued progress or otherwise! You and I have seen God's handwork so far, and I look to him for continued wisdom and clarity as how to handle this next phase. Thank you for your continued prayers for this little four legged friend and companion.

prayer for bentley
-december 6, 2006

Dear Lord,

We got Bentley so that she could be a fun companion to Molly. She did her job when Molly needed her most! Now, however, she is looked at by most of our family as more of a chore than a dedicated and loyal companion.

I am the one who is most attached to her. She needs help, and I love helping her. She is a sweet-faced, gentle-spirited, devoted companion despite her limitations. Am I doing a disservice to her to let her continue to struggle to stand up through her life? I suspect she has many years ahead of her, so it's not like she will just live her life out within a short period. Will she be merely surviving on a daily basis without the ability to run and chase and play and sniff? With a little more time, will you heal her? Will you make her complete once again to pursue her natural activities? That is what she is wired to do not merely to be a companion.

We have been working with Bentley since early September. There has been a significant change, but she still is not able to consistently stay up and walk on all four legs. She is a puppy and wants to play and run fast and she can't. Mentally and physically, it has to be frustrating for her. Or, Maybe it isn't, it is just frustrating for me. She needs someone to help her tend to her needs at night and during the day; I am not always attentive enough to help her to go out regularly.

We are now approaching our fourth month of recuperation. How much longer do I wait? I praise you, Lord, for the progress I have seen and the improvement she has made. But it seems like sometimes we take more steps backwards sometimes than we do frontwards. I wonder now if we are at a plateau. Please Lord give me peace while I wait Let me know when "now" is. A few months back you said "not now." I listened and the lessons you have given me have been remarkable. I need wisdom, Lord. I need you to guide me to the way that you have planned. Whatever that may be. My hands are open, I am trying to not hold Bentley snug in my hands the way I have in the past. It is hard for me to say this and do this but I have released my grip so that *you* can have *your* say. This was a borrowed gift you gave to us in April, and it still is your gift to do with as you please. I am letting go of this and truly giving it to you for approval and direction.

The joy of this dog has been apparent from the beginning. We have continued to find joy in her as she goes forward a few steps and even then back a little. Dogs generate a personality just like people do. She so wants to comply to the rules and requirements. It is not any fault of hers that she is handicapped and is not always able. I suspect if *I* were more consistent and structured, *she* would have a better chance to routinely work through a structured regiment, thus making her stronger in the long run. Maybe that is what I need to pray for; that you would help me be more consistent in my routines in working with her.

Lord, I understand that people are wired so differently, and we all seem to address life so differently. This is not to say that one way is better or worse than another, just different. Some are better at having a plan and sticking to it. I am not one of them. Different bents are reflected in the frustration levels we are able to suppress and variances we are able to overlook. I am very unorganized, so lack of organization doesn't affect me the same way that it would someone who appreciates order. For right now, I am going to try to be disciplined 'til I feel a nudge from you. A plan of daily exercise was suggested as well as a different nightly schedule. I will try to comply. I need your little encouraging reminder to stay on task! Please help me, Lord, to stay focused.

We are a family and there are many components that are wrapped up in our household. Help me to understand if my holding on to hope for recovery in Bentley is your will or mine. Help me to consider the whole family and not just Bentley and my love for her. I know she is *just* a dog and not a child, but she in *now* my dog and I am responsible for her *well*-being. The family loves her and plays with her and helps out a bunch, but because I am home the most, I seem to have the greatest hold of the reigns, so here; I'm giving them to you!

I am so unclear here as to what you want me to do. Please, Lord, direct my path. I am listening. I am waiting and I am confident that you will guide me to your very will for this situation. Amen.

Praise God wherever you are and whatever situation he has allowed you to be in. His glory will shine through!

protection
-december 7, 2006

Bentley's little back feet are all torn up. Sometimes I remember to put on her shoes; sometimes I don't. She has worn out her first pair of tennis shoes, and we are waiting for the back up pair to be delivered (via the Internet). I bought some not so good ones for the meantime and they don't stay on worth a hoot. She needs protection because she still drags when she is excited or wants to go fast or is tired. She just retreats to a front paw pull no matter the pain or the scrapes.

We need God's protection too for without it we tend to drag into a sore spot as well. We get going too fast, or we get to doing something and just don't take the time to think it through. Sometimes we just get tired, and we push it even when we don't have to. We need God to help us stay on a steady pace and be able to walk with a steady gait.

Do not withhold your mercy from me, O LORD; may your love and your truth always protect me.

Psalm 40:11

"Because he loves me," says the LORD, "I will rescue him;
I will protect him, for he acknowledges my name."

Psalm 91:14

Sometimes when I try to slow Bentley down by holding her collar, she turns around and nips at my hand. I wonder, *Do I do that very same thing to God? Do I start nipping when I am impatient about a prayer request? Or when God chooses to deal with a request in a way that I never would have imagined?* We are called to protect our children by using sound judgment when allowing them to do this or that. It is my responsibility to protect Bentley because she will take the "gut" road at any cost and often times so will I.

It is God's responsibility to protect us, and *he will if we ask him and let him.* We let him by obeying him. If Bentley would do as I ask, to walk slow, stay upright, don't drag on the cement, she wouldn't have scrapes and I wouldn't be considered negligent. We too would not have the many altercations we have if we would do what God asks. Life would be so much simpler if I would do what I know is right and not do as I merely want to do. God is never negligent. He is responsible *always*, but *we have to stay on his track* to be under his protection. I know that if I wander off going faster than I am programmed then I am bound to suffer the consequences, and, boy, do I feel those sores. But God is faithful to heal them, and then I start over having once again that choice to make. I have to learn to be content with the pace that God has ordained in my life, and a slow learner am I!

> O LORD my God, I called to you for help and you
> healed me.
>
> Psalm 30:2

> But let all who take refuge in you be glad; let them ever
> sing for joy. Spread your protection over them, that
> those who love your name may rejoice in you.
>
> Psalm 5:11

If God is going to protect me, I have to be still and absorb his protection. I have to put cream on Bentley's feet and then bandage them. It is hard for her to be still. It is hard for me to be still and wait for God. How many times have I just retreated from what I know is to be a "Right" way just because I wanted to do it faster. Scrapes take a long time to heal especially if there is nothing protecting them. Is there a sore spot that you have left unprotected? And no matter how you try to avoid it, the urge to ignore it and hope that it will go away just doesn't happen. It can't heal unless you treat it and protect it.

> He heals the brokenhearted and binds up their
> wounds.
>
> Psalm 147:3

Dear Lord, thank you for your willingness to offer protection to and through my life. I know, often times, I retreat to ways that are not in sound accordance with what I know to be right. There are consequences, and usually they don't sit very comfortably. Please open my heart and slow down my ways so that I will know the lead when you offer it. Let me learn to stay on track at the pace you have declared for my life. Release the hold that pride has on me, and let me patiently adhere to your timing so that I can be securely protected under your authority. Amen.

Praise God wherever you are and whatever situation he has allowed you to be in. His glory will shine through!

we gather
-december 11, 2006

There is an old familiar hymn titled "We Gather Together."
I know many will recognize it. The first line is "We
gather together to ask the Lord's blessing." When you are
struggling with a decision or a day-by-day pull on your
heart, remember to ask God for help and then maybe
confide in a friend. I know that none of us want our dirty
laundry displayed, but there is true comfort in sharing a
concern with someone you trust. It sort of unlocks the room
that you have contained it in and gives it the freedom to be
released. For when we lock things up inside, all we can do is
stew. When we release it from our heart, our mind can start
working on dealing with it, and if you have a dear friend of
confidence, God will allow your words and thoughts to be
launched into a workable solution.

Last week when I sent out a prayer about Bentley,
I had been stewing, and that is the perfect word, just
letting the situation sit there and bubble. Almost upon
immediate release of that e-mail did I feel a terrific
sense of relief and peace and then there were so many
encouraging comments that followed. We are gathered
together to ask the Lord's blessings. We are called to be
encouragers, but we can't encourage if we don't know who
and what needs encouragement. When we shake off the
mask and include others in some of our own concerns,

I think that God is pleased. When we are a team and God sees us working together, it must be such a sight for him to behold. Sometimes don't you think he might say *finally*, you all are working together and have realized the strength and power of many strands rather than trying to keep it together as solo strand.

> The body is a unit, though it is made up of many parts; and though all its parts are many, they form one body. So it is with Christ.
>
> 1 Corinthians 12:12

> For we must all appear before the judgment seat of Christ, that each one may receive what is due him for the things done while in the body, whether good or bad.
>
> 2 Corinthians 5:10

That is the way I think a family is suppose to work too. I think of my own children and how last weekend my son Tom got engaged! He included our whole family in his plan and Rebecca's too and friends too! We were all there in Dallas to watch as he proposed. It was magical, but more than that, it was such a representation of the strength and support that family and friends who are working together exudes.

The first line of the second stanza of We Gather Together is:

"Beside us to guide us, our God with us joining, ordaining, maintaining his kingdom divine."

He is ordaining and maintaining his kingdom, and we are part of that kingdom not merely an isolated element.

Maybe today is a good day to reach out and be a part of the support and strength that is offered by other Christians. Everybody has a something that they are dealing with.

You fit in—either as one in need or one needed. It takes courage sometimes to put a concern "out there," but when you do, I am convinced that God will honor that courage through answered prayers and kind friends.

Now you are the body of Christ, and each one of you is a part of it.

1 Corinthians 12:27

Dear Lord, I just love that line about ordaining and maintaining; for not only do you have a plan but you see it through. May we be team players in your kingdom? May you gather us together, Lord, so that we may represent strength and support in this weary world. Guide us and help us to be listening for our next call from you. And when you do call, let us not hesitate to move—even if it is to go right back to you for the words someone might need to hear or the encouragement or comfort that you would know best how to orchestrate. Thank you for always being so close. In Jesus' name I pray, Amen.

Praise God wherever you are and whatever situation he has allowed you to be in. His glory will shine through!

Part IX

bentley has made the turn

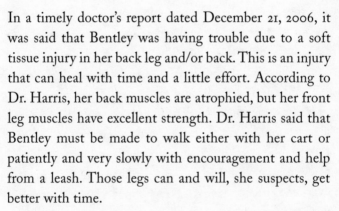

In a timely doctor's report dated December 21, 2006, it was said that Bentley was having trouble due to a soft tissue injury in her back leg and/or back. This is an injury that can heal with time and a little effort. According to Dr. Harris, her back muscles are atrophied, but her front leg muscles have excellent strength. Dr. Harris said that Bentley must be made to walk either with her cart or patiently and very slowly with encouragement and help from a leash. Those legs can and will, she suspects, get better with time.

So we are back to thinking positive and hanging on to the hope that is always available from God himself. My prayer is that God will help Bentley to make the turn for the better.

walk

-january 4, 2007

Bentley had a Dr's appointment a few weeks a go, and the doctor said, "She *can* walk; she is just holding out on you. Put on a harness on her back and make her walk twice a day for at least ten minutes." My hopes were soaring. It was the best news, but that meant that I had to get with it and be consistent in my approach to get her out and exercise her. The doctor said, "She doesn't know that walking will make her better. She just knows it's hard and it is easier and faster to slide on her rear."

Guess you know where I am going with this. Are we able to do a lot more that we are trying to do. I am not talking about taking on new volunteer jobs or finding a job that pays more or being Johnny on the spot for everyone's need. I am talking about your relationship with the Lord. Are you really giving it your absolute best or are you sliding on your rear following the line of least resistance. Like going to church and saying a prayer at dinner. Those are good things, but God is an all time God not just a Sunday God or a mealtime God. He wants to be honored and desired and part of your life at all times in all ways. What are you doing to make that relationship stronger? It is not easy being disciplined. Believe me I am the worst. But I have learned that it is just like anything else. You get what you put into it. If you approach it with sincere desire, you will merit its rewards.

Be strong and take heart, all you who hope in the
LORD.

Psalm 31:24

The name of the LORD is a strong tower; the righteous
run to it and are safe.

Proverbs 18:10

There is no guilt trip here, so please don't think of it that
way. I know that our Almighty God is quietly waiting
with such desire to be available to guide us, comfort us,
and strengthen us by his grace and his mercy and his
wisdom. We are missing an invaluable opportunity if we
continue to pass it up.

Aren't we always encouraging our children to take the
opportunity that is before them? We say, "You don't not
know if it will ever come again." This is your opportunity
today to be on a VIP list with the Almighty God. Find
your Bible, pick it up, and open it anywhere, and start
reading. Talk to God out loud in the car, when no one can
hear or in the shower or when you are getting ready for
the day. It doesn't have to be in some formal setting. God
speaks to you through your mind and heart, but you have
to be able to recognize his whispers. To be able to do that,
you have to know him just like your child recognizes your
voice when you call. He wants us to recognize him when
he calls just as he knows us when we call!

I call on you, O God, for you will answer me; give ear to
me and hear my prayer.

                                            Psalm 17:6

Bentley is up and going. She continues to strengthen her
balance and get stronger in those back legs. But she has
had to be encouraged to take longer walks, go out more
often, and *stop* when she falls on her rear and not scoot
but rather take the time to stand again before moving. It's
has been amazing to see the improvement just because
someone gave me the vision that *she was able to walk.*

But those who hope in the Lord will renew their
strength. They will soar on wings like eagles; they will
run and not grow weary, they will walk and not be
faint.

                                            Isaiah 40:31

Well, you and I are able to better our walk with God,
but we have to be willing to work on it even when it
is hard and keep working so that we become strong in
him. For Bentley, being physically stronger affects every
other aspect of her life.

Being strong in the Lord will affect every aspect of
our lives as well. If you haven't tried this and you just
keep thinking *one day I will give this a shot through I am
not sure it really applies to me,* I challenge you to try it

anyway you want. There is no set pattern. God will honor your desire with his blessings I am sure of it!

Dear Lord, let me not be lazy and slide through life following the line of least resistance. Help me to be willing to "stand up," and not drag through this day or a situation that you have given me. When I come to you, Lord, help me to recognize your hand on my life in every area. Help me to see how a relationship with you does affect *all* areas of my life. I am grateful for the wisdom you share and your grace that is abounding and upon me. I deserve *nothing,* yet you have given me the opportunity for *everything* through the life and death of your son. Let me always be willing to come to you when I am teetering as well as when I am on solid ground. For your hand on my life gives me strength and comfort, and when I am confident of your presence, my gait is steady! Thank you Lord, Amen.

Praise God wherever you are and whatever situation he has allowed you to be in. His glory will shine through!

loyalty

-january 5, 2007

There has been much ado about Bentley because she is the squeaky wheel, and Khaki has pretty much taken a back seat and has just gone with the flow. She does exactly what is asked, ruffles no feathers, and causes no complications. She is oozing with loyalty to Bentley and to us. Many of you who have pets know just what I mean. I was watching her today as I was working with Bentley on walking and Khaki is so accommodating. If Bentley needs to go slow, so does she. If Bentley needs to stop then so does she. When they finish eating she graciously moves aside from her bowl and lets Bentley lick it. She is such a loyal companion to Bentley, and if the roles were reversed, Bentley would not be so patient. Bentley's world is all about Bentley.

I think of how loyal God is to me. How patient and not in a hurry he is. He walks beside me and keeps my pace no matter how slow I am moving. So often, I am on my own agenda. Not taking time to see where God is wanting me to go, rather striving for my own path and direction. Am I as loyal to God as God is to me? Dead flat *no*. I am not, not even a little bit, well, maybe a little bit! But there are still so many times when I don't consider what God is doing or how he would want me to do things or say things. Sure, God nudges me to write these devotionals, and I have great quiet time on most days and pray when I am in the car. But I am still driven by the *me* voice that rides front and center so often. I am the squeaky wheel. I need to grow up and grow out of *me* and into *God's* vision of me instead of my own.

> O LORD, God of our fathers Abraham, Isaac and Israel, keep this desire in the hearts of your people forever, and keep their hearts loyal to you.
>
> 1 Chronicles 29:18

> Devote yourselves to prayer, being watchful and thankful.
>
> Colossians 4:2

Loyalty is a long-standing virtue that comes from pure devotion to someone else. Devotion is caring about someone else more than you do yourself.

I am devoted to my husband and devoted to my family, but that is where I start fading. Devotion takes time, and it is a choice. You are only devoted to someone by choice, that choice is shown in love. Do I love God? Each day I seem to have a stronger devotion. Maybe it is because I have seen the many wonders that only God could have pulled off. Maybe it is because I am learning to shave off the control factor that takes hold of me so ardently and I am realizing that God is the one in control, who am I kidding? Maybe, just maybe I am finally growing up and realizing that God does have *my* best interest in mind and he sees the whole picture. His vision for me just might be a brighter more productive and joyous one than I could ever imagine. I won't know until I choose to devote my *whole* life to him and extend my loyalty day to day to *his* vision. Maybe it is not only a matter of who I devote my life to but also what I devote my life to. For example, if I devoted more time to prayer then it makes sense that I would in turn be showing more devotion to the Lord, for I would be devoted to learning lessons through his word that he has offered me therefore devoting my efforts to him through *him*. What could be better than that?

This is a trustworthy saying. And I want you to stress these things, so that those who have trusted in God may be careful to devote themselves to doing what is good. These things are excellent and profitable for everyone.

Titus 3:8

Dogs are generally loyal by nature to the one who feeds them, loves them, and cares for them. It is not our nature to be loyal to anyone else because we are too busy being loyal to ourselves. I want to be the child whose loyalty to God just radiates from his light that shines within me.

I want to devote my thoughts and actions to *his* direction. So what is holding me back? First of all, I can't do that myself. I have to ask God to come along side me and train me day by day. It will take years and years for it to take, I am sure of it, but why? Might just be as simple as *pride*. It lingers within, causing havoc and destruction to attitudes, relationships, actions etc., and it is definitely false pride for there is nothing in me to be prideful about. For God has been the sole source that has generated any of my successes. *Not me!* If I would just accept that fact— really accept it, then I might have an easier time when it comes to devotion!

> I am saying this for your own good, not to restrict you, but that you may live in a right way in undivided devotion to the LORD.
>
> 1 Corinthians 7:35

> Guard my life, for I am devoted to you. You are my God; save your servant who trusts in you.
>
> Psalm 86:2

Dear Lord, thank you for your unwavering loyalty to finish a work in me that you have started. Thank you for your devotion to the task of molding me in spite of me. Please help me to be reminded that you do see a whole picture not just a part of a picture like I do. Your wisdom is gleamed from your perspective on what has happened, what is happening today and what you have planned to happen. Let me look at you with the awesome appreciation of the God you are and show my devotion and loyalty through my thoughts which transpire into actions. Let my loyalty be reflected in my attitude and my discipline as I strive to know you better and come to you more often. Amen.

Praise God wherever you are and whatever situation he has allowed you to be in. His glory will shine through!

balance

-january 10, 2007

Bentley is now *up* on the hardwood floors. To many that would seem like such a trite accomplishment, but *it is huge*. She has learned balance and combined it with renewed strength. It is funny; I have tried so many things to help keep her bad leg from getting scratched up when she would fall down and drag: shoes, ace wrap, bandages etc. But one day, I found a size small ankle support. It worked wonderfully, but now, what about her toes? She stubs them a bunch. I wrapped them like they do for sports with cotton tape. It was awkward for her at first, but she realized that it didn't hurt to walk because she was protected. It is the little things sometimes right in front of us that can make a big difference in the way we approach life.

> Though he stumble, he will not fall, for the LORD upholds him with his hand.
>
> Psalm 37:24

Balance and strength. That is the combination that would make a tight roper successful. Don't you sometimes feel like you are walking a tight rope, trying to balance everyday activities with the occasional bombs that drop? And don't you sometimes wonder where in the world are you going to get the strength you need to get through the next life obstacle? You *know* the answer. *He* is the simple, right in front of you, solution: *God.* So many times we go out looking for just the right book for advise, or call just the right person for worthy answers, or do just the right thing at just the right time so everything will line up and success will follow. Balance and strength from the Lord is an awesome combination if we would just make that call first.

> Honest scales and balances are from the LORD; all the weights in the bag are of his making.
>
> Proverbs 16:11

Sometimes you have to be able to think out of the box and trusting a God who you can't touch or can't see and can't vocally hear is definitely out of the box! *But God* is real. Let *him* be the fuel that keeps you going. *And* don't take my word for it or anybody else's for that matter. For God to be real to you, you have to *want* him and *ask* him to be part of your life. His reality to someone else has no effect on his reality to you, so don't try to piggyback. *It won't work.* Besides you are either the one who gains or the one who loses... so what is it going to be? God will support you and protect you. (Just a note here on protection.) swald Chambers reminded me of it yesterday when he said, "It is only when we are protected by God with the miraculous sacredness of the Holy Spirit that our spirit, soul and body can be preserved in our righteousness until the coming of Jesus ..." that protection is not just bodily protection but protection of the thoughts in your mind.[6]

He will wrap his word around you and cover you. It might seem awkward at first, but you will soon realize that you can walk a stronger walk. And his support is a lot stronger than an ankle brace or sports tape. The best part is there is no waiting line to talk to him. Close your eyes and think of him and he is there! Amazing that an Almighty, Holy God would be so available to love and care for such an insignificant creature as me! He will care for us right down to our toes! There is nothing to small or too big to bring to God for help.

But let all who take refuge in you be glad; let them ever sing for joy. Spread your protection over them, that those who love your name may rejoice in you.

Psalm 5:11

Kind of like walking that tight rope—how balanced and strong are you? How balanced and strong do you want to be?

Dear Lord, There are so many distractions in this world that do their best to keep us unbalanced. The pulls are from every direction. Quiet our hearts, Lord, so that we may find balance in the very activities *you* have made available for our lives. Let us clearly be able to define your direction as we set forth for our day. Give us your strength through our weaknesses, and balance when we find our world to be unsteady. Let us use that strength and balance to glorify you in all that we do. Amen.

Praise God wherever you are and whatever situation he has allowed you to be in. His glory will shine through!

strength

-january 15, 2007

People ask about Bentley all the time. For a while, we were pretty much the status quo, for as we know, sometimes signs of improvement take a while to recognize. But we walked around the block this week for the first time since last August. It wasn't without stop and rest and a drag here and there but the thing is: we completed the circle. Recuperation is *hard work!* But to be stronger she has to do hard things and go through hard stuff, and no one can do it for her. She has to choose to accept the encouragement from me and be willing in her own stride to proceed.

Do I choose to accept the encouragement of those I love and then am I willing to proceed based on their loving intent? God continually encourages me to do the right thing or respond in a right way or behave in a way that would be an example for someone else, but that doesn't mean I always am willing to follow through. As a matter of fact, the older I get (guess that would be called maturity), the more I realize that I am truly incapable of succeeding without God. I want to do well but the not so well often takes over. Oh, I know what is expected, but I truly do not have the capacity on my own to fulfill it. Do I want to strengthen my mind and body and soul or do I want to remain in the status quo?

CATHERINE JODEIT

Bentley is still a puppy with puppy mentality; she
has puppy energy, puppy smarts, puppy interests, puppy
impulse. Unless I put a leash on her and teach her and
guide her into what is good behavior and how to work
hard to keep strengthening her body, she will just flop
along. This is just *as I do* when I don't accept the leash
that God is leading me with. I might not be a pup, but I
sure have a lot of growing up to do, and I need the help
and encouragement of God to lead my way. God loves me
enough to patiently walk me through the hard times. He
wants me to be stronger and not just be a marshmallow
that melts when the rains come. But my strength cannot
come from me for I have shown my colors on *my* strength,
and when I try to depend on *me* you can count on me
dragging the not so "right" straight on into the mud. My
*right*eousness depends solely on God for he is the only
one who can make me right. For it is through *his* grace
that *my* faith is acceptable, and knowing my track record
of hanging in the mud, I have to have that faith that God
can and will do what he says so that I will be able to carry
on based on *him not me!*

And be found in him, not having a righteousness of my
own that comes from the law, but that which comes
through faith in Christ, the righteousness from God
that depends on faith—

Philippians 3:9

194

God is the only way to get better and be better, but you have to make a choice if *we* want to be *better,* and *the only way* to *be better* is through God and his mercy and his grace and his lead. The leash is a good thing offered by a *good God.* Really, it takes a lot of thinking pressure off of you if you think about it because a leash causes you to stay in step with God and then the decision making is in *his* court and not yours as to the way to go. The Holy Spirit enables us to do what is right and good. Without his enabling we are help*less.*

> And God is able to make all grace abound to you, so that in all things at all times, having all that you need, you will abound in every good work.
>
> 2 Corinthians 9:8

You want to be strong? Then *be strong in the Lord,* and quit trying to be strong in yourself. For God knows what is the best therapy to mold you for *his* loving and useful purpose for others. And whether we accept that fact or not, it is true. We are here on this Earth to be a *blessing* to others. It makes no sense to be a *blessing* to ourselves.

Dear Lord, through the sacrifice on the cross, and the blood that you shed, I have been given a chance to live and forfeit death, which is what my sins deserve. I know that you are a holy and blameless God and that the only way that I am able to come to your throne is through the blood of your Son, which has covered me, and made me acceptable in your eyes. Otherwise the blemished me wouldn't have a change with the *holy* you.

So today, Lord, instead of me thinking of all the ways I have messed up let me reflect with joy on the new life you have given me in you and the new clothes of righteousness that have replaced the rags of my sin. The cross was the foundation; *please,* one day let me truly comprehend that. But for right now, 'til I do, just keep me mindful of what was required to pay my sin debt. I was born with that nature, and you were the only one who could take that noose from around my neck. I am alive in you, and you have made me clean and good through Christ. There are just a bunch of remnants that are still wiggling nerves. I desperately need some help for you to dissolve their hold on me. I know you are working on your own time, and just as improvement in Bentley takes time, so it is with the improvements that you are making in me. Keep tweaking, Lord. I will hang tight to the promise that I have been adopted into your family, and you are a loving, giving, and protecting dad. Please accept my most gracious and humble appreciation, and, Lord, enable me to do the things that seem impossible especially in relationships! Amen.

A note here: many of these thoughts were generated today through lessons from our Sunday school lesson taught by Roger Wernette and our sermon taught by my pastor John Crimmins. I am grateful for the many teachers that God has blessed me with. May he continue to bless them as they boldly declare his word.

Praise God wherever you are and whatever situation he has allowed you to be in. His glory will shine through!

pocket fare

-january 17, 2007

When I take the dogs out walking, I keep the Cheerios in my pocket. These last few days when it has been cold, I keep my hands in my pockets, and Bentley stays pretty close thinking I am going to pull out a treat. She doesn't want to miss out. As a matter of fact, the little piglet wants all of them at once.

What if God did not ration the blessings he gives us? What if he just gave us all his gifts in one great big swoop and we were left to ration? Would we? Or would we be like children at Christmas time and open them all at once, enjoy them for a while, and once again be discontent wanting more. I read a cute e-mail weeks back about someone taking a tour of heaven. First, they were shown the request room, and it was bustling with lots of workers, shuffling to answer the many prayer requests that God had granted. Then there was the processing room, the actual distribution part, busy, busy. And then there was one more area, only a handful of assistants, very quiet, not much action, this was the appreciation room. Sad as it was, it was the room with the least activity. I know it was just a story that someone made up, and it was told in a much better way than I gave it credit for. But it has merited a spot of attention in my heart ever since I read it. How much do we appreciate the blessings God's so graciously bestows? First of all, do we notice them, and second, do we take them for granted and quickly forget to say thank you.

God's holy pockets are full of blessings. Do we walk side by side with God and wait with expectation for the next blessing? I don't want to be like Bentley and walk close just for the favors. I want to walk close in spite of the favors.

Surely you have granted him eternal blessings and made him glad with the joy of your presence.

Psalm 21:6

And when God chooses from *his* pocket fare and gives me a gift he has personally chosen. I want to enjoy it for all that the giver has intended it to be. Blessings are to be appreciated one at a time, not taken for granted or frowned on because it is not enough. Each blessing is *quite* enough and so many of us are overflowing right this very minute with gifts that our Heavenly Father has chosen specifically for our own enjoyment and for our growth. Gifts do not always come wrapped as you would expect them, for oftentimes a gift is presented in simplistic form as Jesus was in the manger. The greatest gifts often come in the most ordinary of circumstance.

From the fullness of his grace we have all received one blessing after another.

John 1:16

Before we ask for more, we might need to make an assessment of what we already have. We are children of God, and he has chosen gifts appropriately for the phase of life we are in. Just as we chose gifts for children of different ages and different stages. May we accept these gifts with gratitude and obedience. May God show us how to use them and how to share them.

"Bring the whole tithe into the storehouse, that there may be food in my house. Test me in this," says the Lord Almighty, "and see if I will not throw open the floodgates of heaven and pour out so much blessing that you will not have room enough for it."

Malachi 3:10

Dear Lord, I am blessed beyond measure. Why me, Lord? Help me not to take for granted the gifts that you have put into my life. Let me examine them through your lens and appreciate them through mine. Let me too, be a giver, Lord, and teach me to walk beside you with appreciation, expectation and also with adoration . Amen.

Praise God wherever you are and whatever situation he has allowed you to be in. His glory will shine through!

CATHERINE JODEIT

compensate

-january 24, 2007

Some days are just easier than others. I took the dogs for a
walk a few days ago, and Bentley was strong. She only had
to stop a few times and seldom lost her balance. Today is
like she is a different dog; she can hardly move one of her
back hind legs. It has been her weakest link throughout
this recovery, must be like arthritis. That hasn't hit me
yet, (having arthritis) but I'm sure its coming. Makes me
realize that some days are just easier than others. It is not
so much what we did or didn't do it's just one of those
life ways.

Don't you find that sometimes it is easier to trust God
than other times? It is easy to give God a parking request
or a get me through this next test request, but what about
giving God the reigns to your children or your spouse or
that friend that hurt your feelings or that partner that took
advantage of you or the employer who seldom appreciates
his employees. Those are the hard ones! Those are the
ones that make getting through life a little tougher. But
what if we looked at it from another angle? With Bentley,
as tough as it is when her leg is weak, she compensates
by taking a little more time to get up and going a little
slower when she finally does. And when all else fails and
an opportunity to jaunt with Khaki arises at the other
end of the yard, she just goes running with those strong
front legs with her rear end dragging.

When days are hard, find your strengths and go with them. When someone asks me what my weaknesses are, I can usually rattle off a pretty good list. But if the question was of strengths? Well, that would take a little longer. Identify what your strengths are and keep them tucked away in an accessible place in your mind so you can grab them when life seems to be causing you to drag. When times are going good, we often tend to leave God out of the picture. Maybe God allows the weak days to pull us back in step with him so that we once again put our trust in him and his strength and might.

God is our refuge and strength, an ever-present help in trouble.

Psalm 46:1

Pick yourself up by the strengths God has given you; natural gifts that you are strong in, capitalize on *them*. That will give the weaker side a chance to catch up. Remember that God is the true source of our strength. For it is in his strength that ours is built. And sometimes it is well to give in to the day and just take a quiet day. Maybe that is truly what your body is begging for and desperately needs. Capitalize on *it*. Take time to listen to God's encouragement as you read the scriptures. Settle into a secure blanket of God's protection no matter what war is raging around you. And above all, take time to praise God for the beauty that surrounds you and his love that encompasses you.

My soul is weary with sorrow; strengthen me according
to your word.

Psalm 119:28

I can do everything through him who gives me
strength.

Philippians 4:13

Yeah, some days are better than others, and some days we
just seem to be stronger than others. But if we didn't have
the weak days then, just as the rain helps us to appreciate
the warmth of the sun, we maybe wouldn't take the time
to even recognize the good days. For they would be old
hat and offer no variety.

Dear Lord, give us your strength when we are weak.
Give us your okay to settle in for a quiet time every once
in a while. May we be looking for the sunshine as we
wade through the rains. And Lord let us be mindful of
our personal strengths that you have blessed us with and
be willing to submit our thoughts to land on those rather
than our weaknesses. Keep our minds strong Lord and
our hearts pure and let us be worthy in your eyes to be a
vessel to spread the word of your love and grace. May we
trust you in *all* situations and not only on days when we
are vulnerable by weaknesses. Amen.

Praise God wherever you are and whatever situation he
has allowed you to be in. His glory will shine through!

Part X

God is good

It is a crooked walk, and it sure looks out of sorts and painful to those who are watching on the sidelines, but God is good, and Bentley is walking and not letting this handicap dampen her love for life and people. The spirit of a lab is personable, for they usually tend to love people. Wherever we go, Bentley is noticed , and most generally, people come up to her to give her some attention because they feel sorry for her. Children and adults as well. She is mobile, and we are grateful, so grateful that God has given her an opportunity to be independent.

inside story
-january 30, 2007

I took the dogs for a walk around the block yesterday. A couple of people stopped and asked if they could help, another stopped to say "poor dog." Bentley has to stop and rest and lots of times that back hind leg just gives way and it takes her a minute to stand back up. What people see on the outside is a dog, who appears to be in pain, struggling to keep up with her friend, Khaki, the older lab. When in fact, what it is, is a success story—a pup with a love for life, filled with energy, and happy to be able to be up on four legs. When she collapses, instead of helping her up, I wait patiently and encourage her 'til she finds the strength and mobility to stand up on her own, then give her a few Cheerios, congratulate her, and again we are on our way. If I lifted her each time, she would not be strengthening those muscles. And she has made so much progress. My point is not about Bentley's deficiencies or progress because what you see on the outside is most of the time *not* the story. For the story is on the inside.

When I look at Bentley, I am not sad but proud. Proud of all the obstacles she has overcome. Proud that God has shown favor on even a dog. Proud to be her master. Proud that we all have hung in there. I think God looks at us and sees the inside story too! The outside is only the cover. It is *his* story after all! He must pleased to watch us as we overcome obstacles and temptations.

He knows that it hasn't always been easy. He also knows that transformation takes time and patience; both of which he has so much to give. He watches as we lift ourselves up and get moving again. He could pick us up himself but he is so often times letting us *try* to strengthen what he knows is within us. He sends encouragement through friends and through his word. Then, when he knows we seemingly have nothing left, he does lift us. But he also wants us to be tenacious and to hang in there when things are hard. Persevere when the world outside says, "Give up." Because perseverance produces character. Character defines what it is that we have inside. He wants us to reflect the true grit of him who is within us.

Not only so, but we also rejoice in our sufferings, because we know that suffering produces perseverance; perseverance, character; and character, hope. And hope does not disappoint us, because God has poured out his love into our hearts by the Holy Spirit, whom he has given us.

Romans 5:3–5

Bentley is standing on all fours and walking, you may think with noodle legs. But she is walking with determination and dog dignity. We know her story, and when we see her walking, we have nothing but gratitude to the Lord for healing her and an appreciation for the hard work she has accomplished to get this far. Remember things are not what they appear to be so many times. Even when things look pretty wonderful on the outside, there is no guarantee that the inside story matches up. Likewise, when things look a little strained on the outside there have probably been many an obstacle that has been overcome. An encouraging word to those whose path God has placed on ours would be like a cool drink on a hot day.

Dear Lord, we all have our stories and obstacles we have had to work through. Thank you for knowing when to lift us up and when to be patient and let us use the muscles you have given us to carry on. Bless us today Lord with your strength. Let us stand up, even if it is on noodle legs, and be your messenger. Help us to overcome obstacles and temptations that have darted out into our paths. Please continue, Lord, to be patient with us for transformation takes a lot of time. Amen.

Praise God wherever you are and whatever situation he has allowed you to be in. His glory will shine through!

keeping up
-february 6, 2007

I have taken Bentley to Memorial Park a couple of times this week by herself. We went on the opposite side of Memorial where it is quiet and there aren't a bunch of distractions. I took her shoe off of her dragging foot and put a leash on her and took her for a long walk on the grass. I just couldn't believe how great she did both times. Then it occurred to me that she has been trying all this time to keep up with Khaki afraid that Khaki might get to a scent before she did and find a treasure in the grass first. When it was just Bentley and me, she was content to stay beside me and walk a slow pace. There was no competition, no threats lurking in the distance, and she was happy just to be my companion. Why is it that we constantly hear that little voice telling us we need to keep up, keep up, keep up?

Someone might be getting more than us, or a treasure might be ahead and unless we are the first in line we'll miss it, or better yet we feel inadequate if someone is moving faster and doing more and getting more. Watching Bentley walk so contentedly and consistently was a reminder to me that as long as I am walking with my eyes on the Lord and not trying to keep up with others around me, there is where my contentment lies. But then I glance away and see something appealing in the distance and here comes the I *want, I want more, I want something that someone else has.* It doesn't necessarily have to be monetary either. It could be a talent or a habit or a personality or even looks. It is that desire to be something that maybe God has not planned you to be or a desire to have something that God has not planned for you to have.

Bentley has limitations. She has limited mobility, but wow, does she have a beautiful face. Next time you glance away from your focus on the Lord and lose a little ground of contentment consider something that you have that maybe someone else doesn't. How about starting with freedom!

Okay, a little more personal: that you have eyes to read, legs to walk, and hands with five fingers. We all have limitations, and that is a good thing. Figure out what they are. Some are glaring insufficiencies; others are subtle insecurities. If we had no limitations, what need would we have for a mighty God? One thing is for sure; we all have temptations that come in the guise of *I want,* and their root is self, and self's root is that old sin nature within us. That nature remains unchecked and unleashed 'til we make a choice to let Jesus put it to death. He is the only way to be free of the torment that arises by the unsatisfied appetite of self. God alone is the one who has no limitations.

Are you content to be walking on the path that God has ordained for you at this time? Am I? Or is the "keep up, keep up" mode of restlessness continuing to take root in your thoughts and rearing its ugly head in your actions? Just go to the park in your heart; find a safe place within you where you are free of the competition and where the peacefulness of contentment has lit a gentle fire. Go from room to room within your soul 'til you find the dwelling place of our Lord. Maybe you have hidden him in an isolated corner and have forgotten his awesome significance. Invite him to share your main room? Be content to walk beside him. Listen for his whispers, and if you are having to try to "keep up", something is wrong because Jesus comes to us where we are and walks with us each at our own pace. You do not have to keep up. You are up, right up there with the Lord. He is bringing you up to his standards little by little!

Since we live by the Spirit, let us keep in step with the Spirit.

Galatians 5:25

Dear Lord, pace me according to your plans. Help me to not run ahead or lag behind but be just where you want to be, going just the speed you want me to go. Let me be contented in my own shoes and in my own spot. When you see that I am glancing away from my focus on you, please, Lord, gently turn my head back to face you. Dismiss the distractions that are pulling at my senses. Use my limitations, insecurities, and insufficiencies as warning lights to remind me to stay close because I need you. Oh, how I need you always! Lord, you have no limitations. How blessed are we that you are mindful of each of us! Thank you, Amen.

Praise God wherever you are and whatever situation he has allowed you to be in. His glory will shine through!

barriers

-february 10, 2007

Each night at bedtime and any time we leave for the evening, we put up the barriers for Bentley. The barriers include three barstools that separate the kitchen from the den. We have done this for months to prevent Bentley from sliding around the house and having a bathroom accident. Well, Bentley is on a pretty good learning curve, and we are pretty much back on the outside schedule for "hurry up's." She has learned to walk on the wooden floors instead of slide and has pretty much accepted her boundaries of the kitchen and the path to the front door. So, for the past two nights I have pushed the barricades back to their rightful place and have trusted Bentley to be in her spot when I came back in the morning. It is working. She continues to be right where I left her in her bed.

What are the barriers that you have put up with some people to make sure they stay within their boundaries? Or maybe the barrier is one you have put up around yourself? This is one of those devotionals that is so hard to write because I am so very guilty or doing this. My barrier is my home. I just love it here. I am surrounded by all of the comforts that fill me up. I have my family, my dogs, my birds, my books, my thoughts, my computer, and it is so very quiet. But there are times when I know I should move on into the world and be active. It is a push sometimes too! But God has not called us to be isolated. He has called us to be fishers of men, and how can you be a fisherman if you aren't out there fishing?

Come, follow me," Jesus said, "and I will make you fishers of men."

Matthew 4:19

We all have something to offer to someone else. Maybe it is conversation, or food, or merely presence, but there is something that we have that someone else needs. As long as we engage in barrier building, we miss the opportunity for God to use us. Sometimes it is just those folks you have barricaded out who God has sent for you to learn *his* greatest lessons from. Usually they are people who aren't "safe" according to your world. They might ask too many questions or have an adverse opinion about something you are strongly involved in or maybe they just seem to know how to kick up dirt in your face. Whenever you feel that barrier mode approaching, ask God to clarify your real reason for putting that barrier up. Is it for protection or for comfort? Maybe that is one in the same. But if it is something that will hurt you or unsteady you, chances are a barrier might be a good thing. If it is put up just because you don't want to be bothered, maybe God might have a lesson for you that you are avoiding. Just think about one of your life stories that might be a worthy share. You may have to become a little vulnerable and take down a barrier, but sometimes taking down a barrier helps the flow—the flow of communication, the flow of friendship, the flow of forgiveness, the flow of diversity, the flow of kindness, the flow of comfort, the flow of God's love within us and to us!

Just one more thought: have you set up a barrier between you and God?

Dear Lord, barriers are a natural inclination for most of us. Let us know when to set them up and when to tear them down. Let us be mindful of boundaries without having structured barriers. Let us not be imposing, rather let us be understanding and patient and willing to submit to the needs of others. Let us embrace the lessons that you are teaching us through adversities, and grow into an attitude of acceptance of your will. May we look to you for bait as we go out fishing. May the nets that you have given us to cast come back full of hungry souls wanting to know you and be loved by you. Amen.

Praise God wherever you are and whatever situation he has allowed you to be in. His glory will shine through!

downs
-february 15, 2007

Mel and I attended a Disciples Seminar last weekend led by John Tolson, founder of The Gathering of Men. This is one of the analogies that he shared. Maybe it's not an analogy, but rather an easy way to remember a significant truth! If football is something that you are familiar with, you will love these simple reminders. I do because they are easy enough for my little mind to remember. How many downs are there in football? If you answered four then *you* are right. Think about these four down truths:

1. God looked *down*
2. Jesus came *down*
3. Jesus lied *down*
4. We are to bow *down*

Bentley was a *down* dog for several months. She couldn't move at all in her hind legs because she was paralyzed. For her to be able to sit *down* or bow *down*, she had to be able to move, and she just couldn't without help from above. Is there something that is paralyzing you from *bowing down?* Do you need a little help from above? For you see, our only part in God's plan is to bow down, and if we commit to bowing down, we lay down our life for God to do as he pleases with us! Jesus Christ laid his life down for us. Now, am I willing to turn around and do the same thing unto the same God who so unselfishly and lovingly made that initial decision about his only son? Are you willing? Am I?

Dear Lord, give us the willingness to bow down to you and look up to your standards. We are unable to be better on our own. We don't have the power to accomplish it even if it is our greatest desire. You are the great *I am,* and I am the insignificant "little me." But, I know, in your eyes, I am great; for *you* are the loving Father who created me and believe me I know the pride of a parent. You have given me four children and added three more (two husbands and a grandchild), and two more on the way (another grandchild, and another daughter, my son is getting married)! I know you know the count, Lord, but I am just acknowledging them and my gratefulness for the gifts that you have given me through them. But I also know as a parent, that though we love our children with all our hearts just as they are, we are always watching patiently as they grow.

Dear Lord, help us to grow in you. Let our growth not be stunted as we cling to the trappings of the world. Let us release our hold on the crutches that give no true significance to life and instead be gripped by your mighty hands and wait for you to lead us. You looked down, sent Jesus down, and Jesus lied down, and all we have to do is *bow* down. Lord, help our knees to bend. Thank you, Lord, Amen.

Praise God wherever you are and whatever situation he has allowed you to be in. His glory will shine through!

stuck

-february 22, 2007

Khaki jumped in on the first step, and Bentley, sidekick that she is, went right behind her into the pool. The problem is that Bentley only got three legs in, the fourth, the weak leg, got stuck on the side. She stayed very still and kept looking around waiting for a rescue. I watched from the inside. Pretty soon, when she felt help was not to come she wiggled around and got all four legs in the water. What does she do now? Again, she was stuck she needed some direction, Khaki is content to walk around the short trail of the first step and Bentley didn't know what to do next! I walked outside and said, "Bentley, you want to go swimming?" And I threw her the tennis ball. Now she had direction, a purpose for being in the pool. She glided herself right off the step and started swimming for the ball. She retrieved it, dropped it, and was ready to play again. She just needed a little nudge of encouragement.

Aren't there times when you get stuck! You just don't know where to go from where you are. The need for direction is apparent but from who? Sometimes I think God is watching from his throne seeing that we are stuck and waiting, just waiting for *him* to come out and tell us the way that we should go or what we should do next. We look around and when no help seems to come forth, we finally move just a little to alter our state of complacency.

God is there. We just haven't acknowledged his presence. We all need a nudge of encouragement. Sometimes God uses others to nudge; sometimes it is something that we read or something that we see, but he is actively working in each of our lives. You wonder how can that be? How can God even know what direction is best for me? How can God make something happen out of nothing? Look at the heavens and the earth. He knows how to make something out of nothing. Look at some of the characters in the Bible One of my favorites is Joseph (Genesis 37 - 39). His brothers were jealous of him; they thought Dad favored him way too much, so they sold him. It sure looked like a bad direction for Joseph, but in the end, the brothers were coming to Joseph in the days of a famine because he held a position of great authority and he was their only hope for help.

Our lives so many times take directions that seem to make no sense. We end up traveling a road that seems to be going nowhere. We end up with frustration, loneliness, and a true anxiety for what life holds ahead. Now do you really think that is what God intends for our lives to be like? *No,* it isn't. Find the road that God is traveling on! His goals for our life are fulfillment, peace, purpose, joy, and above all *love.* If you are feeling unloved and alone, God is your answer. I know he is invisible, and you can't hear his audible voice, and there is nothing tangible to prove his presence, but try talking out loud to him. Ask him to nudge you in the direction that will put you in tandem with *his* plan for your life. I think that so often we are searching for *our* plan, and that is where the static comes in. They are not on the same frequency. God has a specific purpose chosen for your life. It may not seem very significant at this moment, but just like Joseph, God works in stages. He knows your needs and your desires; he is working behind the scenes to get things lined up for *his* timing. He is the road that leads to life, and he wants you right beside him. The question you have to ask yourself is "Do you want to travel with him?"

> But small is the gate and narrow the road that leads to life, and only a few find it.
>
> Matthew 7:14

Bentley was stuck. She needed someone that she trusted to guide her to a purpose. If you by chance are stuck, *ask God* to guide you, and be listening and watching. But remember when you ask, to ask according to *his* will not yours. He is a trustworthy guide, for he has been watching you since your inception, and you are loved, so loved and far from being alone.

Sometimes you need to wiggle a bit so that you are ready when he calls. He will call! Maybe he already has and he's waiting for you to call him back! Be bold with new beginnings. That's where God often starts.

> This is the confidence we have in approaching God: that if we ask anything according to his will, he hears us.
>
> 1 John 5:14

Dear Lord, help us when we're stuck. Nudge us so that we feel compelled to move, not just in any direction but one that is individually suited for who we are and where you want us to be. Show us that we do have a purpose in your kingdom and free us from whatever it is that is holding us down. Each of us are so different, but our basic needs are very much the same. We want to be loved and respected and we want to matter. Remind us everyday of how much we matter to you and how much you love and adore us. But also show us that when everything settles from the frantic pace that we are going and the anxious thoughts that we are thinking that *you are the one who matters the most!* To us! Amen.

Praise God wherever you are and whatever situation he has allowed you to be in. His glory will shine through!

mud holes
-february 28, 2007

I packed up Blake, my grandbaby, and the two dogs, and we were off to the park. A friend had called to meet for lunch, but we decided to meet at the park instead. Just so you will understand, when I walk in the park, I am an explorer. I like taking a different route, troubleshooting when I get to a mud puddle and maneuvering my way over the long sticks that the bikers have purposely placed for jumps. It is a fun jungle out there. This day started like all others. We were off. It is fairly isolated at midday, so the dogs don't have to be leashed. Don't you love it when you don't feel like your leashed, and freedom sets in even if it's only for a little while? The stroller was bouncing as we guided it through the rugged terrain, but that didn't stop the baby from hanging on tight to the animal crackers and goldfish.

After about twenty or thirty minutes into the walk, it had gotten quiet for a moment and the dogs generally stay pretty close, so I looked around to check on where they were, and there she was—Bentley! She had found a cool, deep, nasty, filled with water, hole and she was lying right in the middle of it happy as a clam. There was no yellow showing, she was black from head to toe! My friend was breathless when she saw the sight, and finally, she snickered. All I could do at that point was say, "Come on, Bentley!" I couldn't be mad at her!

Life is just a walk in the park. Everyday we explore new beginnings, new surroundings, new ventures, shady areas, surprises, and *mud holes*. Sometimes you can side step them, and sometimes there is no getting around them. You just have to go through them. God knows where the mud holes of our lives are. Some, we have gotten ourselves into because we simply weren't paying attention to the path that we were on. Some just ended up right in the middle of our path, and there was no escape route. And some are mud holes that someone else stepped in and have splashed the dirt right on us. However we have been affected by the grime; there is one thing that comes from it: clean me up!

There is no mud hole so deep or so dirty that God can't come in and clean us up! *None!* Nothing is too big or too hard or too dirty! The dirt can be as slight as gossiping about others or being unkind to a friend or family member or abandoning a need of another for selfish purpose of yourself. Or it can be as big as an unsightly scar on your heart from a childhood wound or a way of life that has yet to be uncovered or an unhealthy habit that is stuck in your lifestyle, or a tragic mistake that you have made. Whatever it is: we worship a loving God who understands the blemish and is the only answer to removing it. Try as we may we just can't shake it ourselves.

Christ ended up in a mud hole that cost him his life. His body was covered with his blood to account for our grime. He was willing to go to the cross to be the clean up for all of us. So when you evaluate your mud hole, remember the power wash of Christ and realize that you have been freed from the grime. You no longer have to contend with the dirt. If anyone is reading this today and has not asked Christ to be their savior, close your eyes, right now, and ask him to be a part of your life beginning now. It's not like you have to wait in line or find just the right time and place to talk to him. God is waiting; he has been for a long time. Invite him to be a part of your life. You might not feel any different when you open your eyes, but I guarantee you your life *will never be the same!* God will cleanse your life and renew your spirit with a heavenly power that will finally allow you to be at peace with yourself.

Regarding the mud hole Bentley found, you aren't going to believe this, but as we were coming out of the forest, there was a hose hook up right there in front of us. I had never seen it before. Maybe it was a left over from the trail riders when they came for the rodeo parade, but there it was a working hose, and you know the rest. I did have a blanket in the car that they ride on, but a wet blanket sure beats a muddy one!

Dear Lord, you do know where the mud holes are in our lives. You probably know of ones that we haven't recognized or haven't wanted to recognize. I know that we have been cleansed by the blood of Christ, but it is so refreshing each day to wake up and realize that this too is a new clean start from yesterday. Forgive us, Lord, when we intentionally play in the mud. Help us to learn to sidestep when we see a pit in front of us. Thank you each day for the thoughts you put in my heart to share.

May they be a blessing and a word to those who you have chosen to read them. Glory be to you, our Lord, God, and Savior! Amen.

Praise God wherever you are and whatever situation he has allowed you to be in. His glory will shine through!

helpers
-march 2, 2007

When the Lord puts at least two examples of the same topic on my heart in a short time frame, I have learned to listen. The topic is "hearing"! Last week I took Bentley to the vet for a tune up. The waiting room was full so I took Bentley back outside 'til some of the folks and dogs cleared out. A few minutes later, a middle-aged stout and ruddy-faced man came outside dressed in his scrubs. The office apparently had told him that we might need some help getting inside. We didn't but he was insistent on helping. People feel so sorry for Bentley when they see her limping. I had told him that she was okay, but he would have nothing to do with that. He was going to carry her in.

When we settled into the examine room , I realized that this man could neither hear nor talk. I asked him if he could read lips and he made the "little" sign with his fingers. I told him thank you for the help. He smiled and shook his head up and down. I thought about that man all week, still am thinking of him. I wonder how he ended up with that job. Who got him there? What made them hire him? He couldn't hear and he couldn't talk, but he could help and help he did with a smile of gratification.

We *can* hear and we *can* speak. But how many times do we help someone who is in need? I think about a lady whose groceries have spilled, a mom carrying a baby trying to open a door with her hands full, a handicapped person who is trying to get into a crowded elevator, or arranging meals for someone who is sick. There are a million scenarios. We all have the ability and the means to help—some of us a lot, some of us only a little. But we all do have something to give in spite of *our* limitations. This man at the vet's office was so gentle with Bentley and Bentley wasn't scared of him, yet he never said a word. What if we couldn't talk? Would our demeanor portray a gentleness in spite of the silence? Would the satisfaction that we would get from helping another fill us up? I suspect that this job has given this man a self-respect in spite of *his* many limitations. I cannot imagine living in a world of silence and only being able to communicate by hand prompts. Just think how different your world would be if you couldn't hear? How would you compensate?

If one falls down, his friend can help him up. But pity the man who falls and has no one to help him up!

Ecclesiastes 4:10

I went to a dinner tonight for the Center for Speech and Hearing. It was their sixtieth birthday. They were honoring some of the people who had dedicated so much of their time and financial contributions to the school. There was a little girl who was a co-emcee with Tom Koch. She was twelve and her name was Anna. At the age of six months, she was diagnosed with a severe hearing loss. At the age of eighteen months a cochlear implant, a hearing devise was put inside the back of the head which activates vibrations to the ear bypassing the standard way of hearing which was damaged. This devise enabled her to hear and to learn to speak. She won first place at a spelling bee at her school this year and went on to win fifth place in the district. She was a darling emcee! You couldn't help but imagine how much she has overcome to be mainstreamed as she is and to be so confident and personable.

There were lots of people behind the scenes who have helped her but it all started with the recognition of a problem and the help of her parents. . These men and women who were honored tonight have been solid rocks who have promoted and secured a vision and a mission for this school; the cochlear implant had to be backed by education. Helpers, we all are helpers somewhere and hearers, most of us are hearers, but are we doers with what we hear? Help is started by the help that we are given from God and then we are to pass that help along.

> For I am the LORD, your God, who takes hold of your right hand and says to you, Do not fear; I will help you.
>
> Isaiah 41:13

For this man at the vets office and for little Anna, it is those folks who have helped them along the way that have enabled them to exhibit their purpose. We are those people behind the scenes. We are called to get out there and help. We all have a purpose on this Earth, and our purpose is doing what God has called us to do. Each of our ways will be different because we are so different. May we overcome our limitations, handicaps, and insecurities and be the help we are called to be, to someone who is in need.

Dear Lord, thank you for the ears that you have given us to hear. May we hear sounds that touch our hearts. May we listen, really listen to others when they speak and may we discern a need even if it is not voiced. Let us not be in such a hurry that we don't stop for someone who needs a hand. Let us be the behind the scenes folks who make a difference for your kingdom while we are on this Earth. Thank you, Lord, for the gift of hearing. It is something that we take for granted each day. Amen.

Praise God wherever you are and whatever situation he has allowed you to be in. His glory will shine through!

Part XI

spring hope

Spring is a time of new beginnings ...Bentley continues to truck along and every once in a while I see what I hope to be a little more improvement. It might just be in my mind because any change is so small and so slow. But I continue to hope that she will get better, and her muscles will get stronger and her co-ordination will get better....... but I have to say I am so very grateful for what we have. Because if I take the time to look back as to where we have been and where we have come ...the journey has taken on many a milestone!

dead tree
-march 5, 2007

The past few days have just been beautiful, and every afternoon I've taken my little four legged friends for a walk in the park. Last week we were trying to work our way through the woods and we cut through the forest to get from one trail to another. It is always fun to veer off the beaten track a little. There was a big tree that had fallen on the path that we were taking. Khaki hopped right over it; I walked over it and then there was Bentley. There she stood perfectly still, looking at the fallen tree. It wasn't so easy a task for her and she knew it! Khaki and I had both stopped and we were waiting and watching her. This was a huge stumbling block! I thought about lifting her over it but then realized that she can do this! So I told her in a sweet voice "Bentley, you can do this, come on and get on over it." It really was funny. She looked back at the tree then back at me, and once again, I repeated what I had said. She had to make a choice, for she could see that I was holding my ground, literally, and she was on her own. She jumped over with those front two paws, then jumped like a rabbit with the back ones. *She did it!* Yeah, Bentley!

Isn't that the way life is; you are walking along minding your own business enjoying the stroll of life and there it is: a stumbling block. And it is not generally an easy one to hurdle. You look at it, evaluate it, try to find a way around it and you finally face it. You have to get over it! Is there something in your life that is a true stumbling block? Something that you need to get over but continues to be a huge distraction in your mind and on your path. Maybe it is a somebody instead of a something! Or a situation that looks hopeless and you are *dwelling on it* instead of *praying over it.*

Whatever it is, you have to get over it and move on. God is right there to quietly whisper the encouragement you need to hear. Listen to your heart. That is where he is. That is where he lives. You can do it. Don't let this one obstacle stop you from pursuing your dream, rob you of the joy of the day, or convince you to turn back. You can do it. You have the power of our mighty God right beside you. Ask him to help pole vault you over the log that is blocking your path. Don't get stuck in the forest because of one dead tree! And when you finally do get over it … you find yourself saying, "Yeah, God"Because after all, it was his power that got you over it.

Jesus turned and said to Peter, "Get behind me, Satan! You are a stumbling block to me; you do not have in mind the things of God, but the things of men."

Matthew 16:23

Bentley continues to be a hard worker, but it is most humbling that she is so dependent on what I say to her and how I say it. I guess she knows that I have hung with her through some pretty rough times. Who has hung with you when times have been tough? Family and friends are wonderful but there truly is no one who is as wise, as loving, as concerned, as persistent, or as genuinely interested in your life and your well-being as Jesus is. He loves you, loves you, loves you and each day has chosen to walk right beside you and me too! Sometimes I pay a lot of attention to him and sometimes I don't. But boy when I do, it is a true and glorious walk in *his* PARK. You *know* what I mean, things just go better with God.

Dear Lord, let us look at a fallen tree for what it is, *dead!* Help us to not dwell on it but give us the courage and the wherewithal to get over it. There are always going to be distractions in our lives that are most unhealthy, and our human nature is to milk them 'til they're dry. Help us to not put the time and energy into something that has no true value or purpose in our lives. For when we submit to the stumbling blocks, we are not trusting you to be the Almighty God that we know you to be. There is nothing so big or so hard that you cannot deal with it and turn it into something good and precious in your sight.

You are the *God of the universe.* If you can make an earth and the skies and the moon and the sun and everything under the heavens, you too can surely work on sorted relationships, obstinate diseases, and futile wars across the nations and our own personal stumbling blocks. I pray, dear Lord, that those who are reading this today will submit their stumbling distraction into your hands whatever it may be. And I pray, Lord, that you will lift them over that block and help them move on. Amen.

Praise God wherever you are and whatever situation he has allowed you to be in. His glory will shine through!

life biters
-march 30, 2007

There were flocking by the hundreds and Bentley and I were both in a frenzy trying to escape their busy, biting, engulfing presence. We had gone to Memorial Park. I choose different areas all over the park to walk, but today, I had chosen the biking trails. We hadn't been there in a while and usually it is my favorite because it is deep in the woods and just beautiful. Wrong choice! The mosquitoes had taken over. It clearly was their territory, and we had entered it. Truly, it looked like someone had splattered tiny dots of black paint on each of us from head to toe for they had descended in droves from out of nowhere. Khaki, the old dog, had run ahead. She knew how to escape. Oh, how I wish I would have chosen a different path, or had I known, I would have used some insect repellent.

What do you do when a flurry of life biters descends on you? Life biters, things that come out of nowhere and eat at your peace. Relationships, health issues, moods, an orchestrated plan falling short of expectancy. Life biters are anything that cause you discomfort or worry or allows you to be saturated with fear, shame, distrust or discontent. So many times, we can look back and say, oh, I wish I would have chosen a different path. Maybe you got angry with someone, didn't listen to valuable advice, or tried to do things too quickly. Now, all you want to do is escape the situation and not turn back. There is always a way out or a way through. It might not be pretty and it might take a little humility, but you can depend on God for guidance to get you through. He doesn't always protect you from the bite because sometimes the bite is just what he uses to get your attention. Been bitten lately?

God's grace covers my iniquities but he also allows me to make wrong choices and go through the swarm of biters. For it is then that he clears the way for us to have a more peaceful, resolved walk of life. It seems that it is when we are forced to tackle the swarm of biters that that is when we are finally desperate enough to pursue a relationship with God that he has quietly been inviting us to for years.

From the fullness of his grace we have all received one blessing after another.

John 1:16

But to each one of us grace has been given as Christ apportioned it.

Ephesians 4:7

Bentley was overwhelmed and just started sliding on her rear because she thought that was a much faster mode of transportation. "Get up Bentley! Get up we need to get out of here." Finally, she struggled back to all fours, and we were finally headed towards the clearing. Do you find yourself sliding through rather than standing tall and using all that you have got to proceed through the darkened maze? Try to evaluate what you do have. What are you standing on? Who are you standing with? We have the ability to tap into the greatest power on Earth, and it isn't your power and it isn't mine. It is Jesus Christ, clear and simple. The maze, yeah it is often times overwhelming but God knows the way out and he can and will protect you and I, as we stand tall on his shoulders and walk through it. He *will* be the shield.

> Every word of God is flawless; he is a shield to those who take refuge in him.
>
> Proverbs 30:5

Next time you are bombarded by life biters, go to the one who can protect you. In our case of the mosquitoes, I just know that God must have finally come to help Bentley. She was too heavy to carry, but God knew how to get her going. God knows how to get me going too. I first must want the help, then I must follow his lead.

Dear Lord, thank you that you know how to get our attention, and though you know that it is a temporary hurt, you also know where it will lead. Protect me from life biters and protect me from *being* a life biter. Let me tap into your great and mighty power and help me be humble enough to recognize my need for protection; your protection. Dear Lord, light the fire of advance under my feet when you see I have stalled out. Keep me going in your direction and help me to recognize your path as I travel through the forests. Amen.

Praise God wherever you are and whatever situation he has allowed you to be in. His glory will shine through!

letter to dr. harris and to dr. doyle

-april 2, 2007

Dear Dr. Harris and Dr. Doyle,

Thank you for all the time, encouragement, professional advise, and therapy that you have given to Bentley since last September. You both have been wonderful as well as your precious assistants. You have walked with me down an emotional path and have, through your professional efforts, gotten Bentley to a point of walking and now swimming.

I thank you for being positive, not really knowing if anything would take or help. Thank you for trying, and for having faith in a young dog and a timeless eastern practice of acupuncture, herbs and physical therapy. You were steady, and you were so sweet to Bentley each time she came for an appointment. You worked well as a team and you beat all odds.

She continues to have a weak leg, but her spirit is still puppy strong. She is happy to get to go to the park each day and I still think that maybe with time she will continue to get even stronger. Dr. Doyle, we have tried to walk on the banks of the ditches to strengthen her upper legs, and Dr. Harris, she seems to love the swimming and is working all of her legs. We can work with what we have got no doubt. She is able to spend time outside, and she seems to have a lot more control over bathroom chores. She is even wagging her tail slowly. The bone on her upper spine still seems to be arched, so I guess the muscles in her legs still need some work. I am ever hopeful that she will continue to progress.

I cannot thank you enough for your heartfelt treatments and patience not just with Bentley but also with me. A book entitled *Raising Bentley* is being considered for publication, and I have two other books to be released this year, one entitled Sweet Sixteen with Hodgkin's, the reason for Bentleys debut in the first place. The Bentley book will be on next year's agenda. I think you all are just wonderful and sincerely appreciate your professional treatment of Bentley. I am sure all animals that you see get well above an average commitment, for you all gave your best effort and it showed in all ways, through your attitudes and Bentley's response.

You all have been wonderful to us. Thank you for treating Bentley and giving her her life back. As you know, seeing her paralyzed after such a sever spinal cord injury was something that broke my whole family's heart. And now, we are back, and Bentley is able to live life in her little wobbling way, and we are ever grateful for her recovery. We thank you so very much for your efforts. God has blessed us through our prayers and through you the professionals who gave her your best to make her better.

May God Bless you,
Cathy Jodeit

drop
-april 17, 2007

"Get the ball, Bentley; get the ball." She slivers into the pool because the damage to her back hind leg is still very apparent. And there she goes with a steady paddling gait to fetch the tennis ball that floats across the length of the pool. A great swimmer and glad to be back in the pool, we were told that water might be her greatest mode for healing. We are still hanging on to hope that one day she will be full throttle again. She opens her mouth wide, grabs the ball, and with great satisfaction and success heads back to her home base, the top step. "Drop!"

Can't do it!

"Drop, Bentley."

Still can't do it, or maybe a better phrase is won't do it. So I tug at the ball while it is still securely planted in her mouth but still no avail. I can't get the ball unless she releases it. I know she still wants to play, but it is hard for her to give up something that she has struggled so hard to pursue. There is a bit of pleasure with each clutch as she turns it to and fro in her mouth.

What is it that you are holding so tightly too? What is keeping you on the step and holding you back from going forward and moving on? We all have those things we just sit and chew on and to no avail. We don't make them better or even easier to swallow they remain a sustained nuisance that keep us busy gnawing, honestly knowing that *we* aren't going to change them. Think about people and circumstances and situations that we fret over. If we would just let go, life could go on. Why won't Bentley let go? Maybe because she wants to hold on and savor the prize.

Am I holding on to something considering it a feat? I have to admit that sometimes I hold on …because I can, and it gives me a semblance of power or control. Not because it benefits me in any real way. It actually, if the truth were known, is to my detriment. For it keeps me entangled, self-dependent, and distracted. And it stops me from moving on with the rest of life. God is standing on the step, with his hand extended. Give it to *me.* Quit chewing needlessly on something that has no merit. Put it in *my* hands, and let *me* be in control of it. *Trust me!* We only have to be willing to give it up to God for he will take care of it.

[Jesus Comforts His Disciples] Do not let your hearts be troubled. Trust in God; trust also in me.

John 14:1

Finally, after much ado and chew, Bentley releases her trophy and with grateful anticipation looks forward to next throw. May we too, with God's help, release what we have been chewing on and look forward to God's next throw.

Dear Lord, release me from the needless worries that I am chewing on. They almost seem addictive sometimes, and I feel powerless to open my hands and heart to release them. Let me open my fists and hand them over to you. Help me, Lord, to enjoy this precious life that you have given to me and to not fret over things which I really have no control over anyway. Let me trust you and open handedly and willing release people and situations that I know you have got a plan for, and that I have no true control over anyway. Lord, I know you are so much more capable than I could ever imagine you to be. Let me trust you and believe in you with all of my heart and soul and mind. You are the almighty God of this universe and there is nothing, nothing, nothing, that you do not have authority over. Amen.

Praise God wherever you are and whatever situation he has allowed you to be in. His glory will shine through.

anticipate joy
-april 26, 2007

Bentley saw the leashes and knew the drill. We hadn't been on a good walk in a couple of weeks. We've been working on swimming instead. She could hardly stand it. Bless her heart, she was trying to jump and kept dragging in circles and her mouth seemed to convey the happiest smile. The anticipation alone was enough to fill her heart.

What are you anticipating? A summer trip, a new job, a lunch invitation, a new baby, a redo in your house, a move, a wedding, the end of a project, a new deal, a vacation, a sporting event, a child's graduation? These are all *look forward* to things! What about those things that you anticipate with trepidation? The have to's. An employee's evaluation, taxes, a social function that you are obligated to attend, a drive across town in five o'clock traffic or even going the grocery store run. With either scenario, your emotions are sure to be tapped. But I want what Bentley felt—that all out, filled with joy, this is the best day ever emotion. It should be. Everyday should be a day of celebration. But we so often take for granted just the blessing of waking up and being able to walk to the shower, have breakfast in the kitchen, and have someone around us who cares. We are a privileged society. We have the recourses to explore new venues, seek out adventure, try new things, and build new relationships. But so often we accept mediocrity and don't strive for the best for our lives. Wake up! Let's wake up and smell the roses or the coffee. This is a new day. There are great things to see, great people to meet, great places to go. Shake off the restless stagnant everyday lifestyle and shake your world up a little. Let's find the joy that God has provided for us in the little things that surround us. Anticipate *joy!*

A cheerful look brings joy to the heart, and good news gives health to the bones.

Proverbs 15:30

We were walking at Memorial Park yesterday along the railroad tracks. There are several ways to look at that area. There are weeds and grass that hasn't been mowed, and a chopped up deserted gritty road and mud puddles from the rains were scattered along the grass, but there were the most beautiful bright orange butterflies hovering the purple wildflowers. The contrast of the clear, blue-sky backdrop with the fluttering brightly colored butterflies was more than amazing. The butterflies were the focus not the weeds. And the purple flowers, I mean here they were, where you would least expect them. No one came out and purposely planted them. God chose their spot, and grew them there! God chose your spot …and is growing you right there!

Each time we walk in the park, there is something new to explore. This is the way it is with our lives if we would just anticipate with joy something new to explore. Look at some of those situations that you are approaching with dread and instead of going with anticipation of dread try anticipating with hope.

Consider your spot ...maybe you are surrounded by weeds but *you* can be the beautiful focal point. Whatever spot you are in there is a potential for joy. Sometimes you have to look a little harder through the weeds. Enjoy this day that God has given you. Instead of complaining of the mediocrity of everyday living, celebrate your life and the life of those around you. Find the joys of the little things. Be looking for the joys of the little things. They are everywhere! If only we would look with different eyes, we would see the many blessings that surround us.

Dear Lord, thank you for this day. Thank you for my little crippled dog who continues to be a reminder of true joy. For even in her circumstance, she is content and celebrates the joy of friendship, food and a field (literally) trip. Let me too appreciate the little things that you have provided in my life and let me celebrate the life you have given me. Let me anticipate *joy!* Amen.

Praise God wherever you are and whatever situation he has allowed you to be in. His glory will shine through!

mimic
-april 27, 2007

I was in the front yard with my three little friends yesterday—Blake, thirteen months and walking, and my two labs, Bentley and Khaki. Blake had his little walker and was strutting his stuff walking down the street as the dogs followed on the grass. Bentley still needs reminding to "get up", so every once in a while, I would say, "Up Bentley." And she would pot up. "Up Bentley!"

Then as we walked a little further, I hear, "*Up*," and again, "*Up*." And I looked back and sure enough Bentley was down again, but this time it was Blake who was telling Bentley to get up. He has heard it said and watched it done so often that he was mimicking me. This was not on my list of what to teach my grandbaby! But this makes me realize how much he picks up by watching and listening, and the thing is, I unconsciously am teaching as I just go about everyday living. I am an example that little eyes are watching, closer than I would like!

Mimic—what a funny word. But all of us do it. We mimic a style of clothes, we mimic the way someone talks when we have been around them for a while, we mimic behavior and mannerisms, and we mimic traditions. We pick so much up from our surroundings and the people we chose to hang with. It is the subtle influences that unknowingly latch on to us. Be on guard. Guard you mind and your thoughts and your actions. We need to have some internal detector to beep when we are slipping into a compromising mode that falls short of what we know is right. Oh, wait; we already do have a detector. Our conscience guided by the Holy Spirit. But the question is: is the switch on or off?

Christ has given us an example to live by. He is the only influence who remains pure and untouched and unswayed (I know that is not a word but I liked it) by the world and all its trappings. He is our internal detector, and for our own good and productivity, we would be remiss if we didn't have that switch on *on* at all times. For it is our reminder to mimic Jesus. He wants us to watch close, listen attentively, and mimic his actions. He is a terrific leader, the best as a matter of fact. He wants his ways to be so embedded in our hearts and minds that we unconsciously act and react to situations just as he would. Just as peers and children and friends are consciously watching us, we too have to keep watch and have our eyes focused on Christ for direction for wisdom and for the example of how to proceed through life.

Be on your guard; stand firm in the faith; be men of courage; be strong.

1 Corinthians 16:13

There have been many a person in my life who has influenced me, most of them good, just a few not so good.

The older I get, the more I am aware of the standards I have chosen to live by. Some still need to be altered no doubt, but some tend to be gaining momentum and I can feel the Lord's influence and encouragement. As long as I stay close and focus on him, he will lead me in his direction and his influence will continue to have an impact. I just need to keep that switch on *on* and be mindful to listen and react when it beeps. For when we acknowledge the beep we are acknowledging his way. And when we choose to mimic the way of the Lord, don't you think it must fill his heart with great delight!

Dear Lord, we are influenced everyday by the subtleties of this world and the people who are around us. Help us to see through the masks, and the false opportunities that hold no true merit to our lives. Let us come to know you so intimately that we do react and respond through your nature that lives within us. Be our internal detector and warn us when we get off course, and, Lord, let us not have the sound on so low that we are able to ignore it. Let it be a warning alarm that we recognize so that we will make way for a change of course. Lord, help me to be an influence on this Earth in all situations that would reflect my love for you, and please especially when my grandbaby is around, let him see the you that lives in me. Amen.

Praise God wherever you are and whatever situation he has allowed you to be in. His glory will shine through!

crutch
-may 7, 2007

The rains had left some muddy puddles on the side of the tracks that we usually walk on. So we crossed the street to the grassy open meadow across the street. Bentley's back leg must have been hurting pretty bad because every time she would get on all fours she would collapse again. Bless her heart, I knew she wanted to be out and Khaki too was so anxious for a walk. So I told them to stay (I could still see them), and I walked back to the car and got out the old towel that I had in the trunk. I rolled it up and made a sling under Bentley's stomach, and we were off. The dogs stay pretty close to me on a walk anyway, but this side of the road was new territory so they didn't know which way to go. I was having to walk beside Bentley as I was lifting her so I was unable to lead. We walked without our usual determined candor, and the whole time you could tell they were a little hesitant and constantly looking to me for direction.

When was the last time you ended up in new territory? Didn't you find yourself needing a leader, someone who knew the way? Now don't get me wrong, I am all for exploring but sometimes the territory is darkened with doubt, fear, and uncertainty. The way is not clear and neither is the destination. So often, we try to hobble through it alone and we collapse with exhaustion because we just don't have the stamina, emotionally and physically to wander through the vast meadow which seemingly has no end. I wonder sometimes, why I wait to ask for a leader *the* leader …to be my guide. Maybe it is because I am so overwhelmed that I just don't seem to be able to gather my thoughts. From what I have learned, it is not that I don't *know* that God can and will walk with me through it, rather that I just haven't asked.

> Now to him who is able to do immeasurably more than all we ask or imagine, according to his power that is at work within us, to him be glory in the church and in Christ Jesus throughout all generations, for ever and ever! Amen.
>
> Ephesians 3:20–21

Now really, if you are, or if I am in the midst of a challenge that seems way out of our bounds or over our heads, it would be a smart move to *ask* God for direction, don't you think? So what is holding me back? The usual answer is pride! It goes back to that familiar two-year-old response: "*mine.*" We want to do it ourselves; we want to squirm around and be the sole achiever without the help and assistance of anyone else especially a God who we can't even see.

We want the glory and we want to pat ourselves on the back, and say, "I did it! It was me. I got through it! Oh, it was hard, and I struggled but I conquered it." The reality is God was with you all along, whether you recognize him or not is merely your interpretation. The advantage of asking God for help is to our advantage not his. For when we intentionally go to the Lord and ask, we are consciously submitting to *his* will and not ours. We are putting the new territory situation in the hands of an old timer familiar with every pothole and prickly step of the meadow. He is willing to carry us over and through the mire, and somehow, he will ease our journey. Maybe it is through his comfort or the peace of knowing he is there in spite of the circumstances or just having a companion in the midst of true loneliness. You will not only be aware of his presence, but become dependant on it. Allow God just once to help you, and you will be hooked and always be looking again for his wisdom and guidance. For God is good and God is great, and his reputation precedes him.

Bentley needed a sling; I need a crutch! Next time you feel like you have hit some new territory way out of your bounds, ask God to be your leader and let him be the crutch to help get you through. A crutch is often looked at as a hindrance when in actually it is what helps to give us the strength to move on. Think crutch, think God.

Dear Lord, I am nuts to think I can do life on my own! I struggle through decisions, relationships, and new territories everyday, and without you Lord, very little progress is made. Help me to realize that my potential when I have you by my side in no way compares to my aimless living without you. I ask you today to lead me in whatever direction you have planned for my life. Let me follow you with a willing heart and mind. Let me realize the value of you being my crutch and know that it doesn't weaken who I am but only glorifies who you are through me. Amen

Praise God wherever you are and whatever situation he has allowed you to be in. His glory will shine through.

self-conscious

-may 17, 2007

Bentley's face is full of delight each time I tell the dogs that we are going for walk. Khaki and Bentley hurry to the gate. It always takes Bentley a little longer because she gets so excited that it is hard for her not to drag. Even in her fastest mode of getting around, it still isn't fast enough. We go to the car, wait to put the blanket in the back seat, and then I help Bentley in by counting to three; she jumps with her front paws and I lift her back end by her tail. Then Khaki climbs in slowly to the floor, and we are set.

Bentley knows when we are right around the corner from the park, and she starts making noises that sound a little like gospel singing (you know when the notes are held for a long time) because she knows we are close. Then I open the car door, and she just can't wait for help she hurries and flops out like a seal would, right on the grass. Khaki follows. And the walk begins. She has a hard time at first because every few steps her back leg seems to collapse, and she has to regroup and stand again. By the end of the walk, she is able to stay up pretty good.

My point for the story is Bentley is not self-conscious. She thinks just like Khaki thinks. *We're going for a walk, and I can't wait.* Though she is aware of her limitations, she doesn't dwell on them. She moves forward with anticipation and has a true desire to have fun, and she does. She has just as great of a time as Khaki does: open fields, great smells, people to watch, and a friend by her side (well most of the time). We all have limitations and things that make us self-conscious. Sometimes they are physical, like weight or gait or a birthmark or having to use a crutch to help you get around or needing a wheel chair because you need a mode of transportation. (I'm thinking of my friend Kitty who has to stay off of her leg for several months due to a terrible femur break.) Sometimes they are mental; you don't think that you belong in the group that you are in, you are embarrassed because you don't seem to have much to offer, or you just don't feel like you measure up.

Whatever the limitations are, we all have some of them. But the critical question is this: is our focus on *us* or on the God who made *us*. It is one of the hardest things for me to do, but when I start feeling that way, I have to go back to the truth: God created me and he doesn't make mistakes. I am just fine in God's eyes, as a matter of fact, he is pretty proud of his work. For it is not about looks or personality or gifts and talents. It is about who you are as a whole and how you are going to play out the *who you are with what you have*. As long as the focus is on you and on me then we are not making ourselves totally available *to* God. For we have been put in each of our spots *by* God *for* God for his purposes.

Sometimes we have to back up and go to the spot of truth and disregard all the lingering thoughts that are rolling around in our minds about our inadequacies. The truth is we are okay. We are better than okay because the mighty God of the Universe created us, and we have potential. I suspect there is a bunch of undiscovered potential in each of us, but we are so busy being self-conscious that we are restrained in seeking it. . We find ourselves steeped in a subjective mode rather than an objective mode; we tend to be thinking about ourselves instead of thinking about God. Doing things or thinking from our mental standpoint rather than putting the emphasis of our life on what God wants.

I want so to be free of what people think and what I think people are thinking (it takes up so much energy, and I seldom get it right anyway) and just do what is right in the eyes of the Lord. For in the end his evaluation is all that matters. I want to approach life like Bentley—with joyful anticipation not paying any attention to my many limitations. To be able to just go about, doing my best with God in mind rather than dwelling on some insecurity that Satan is using as a terrific distraction. I might not be all things to all folks, but I am all I've got and that is more than enough for God.

We each have been planted in different gardens of life for his reason. We can't stay tucked into the soil forever for he has a magnificent display of his glory in mind, and we are part of it! Enjoy life today! For it is through our limitations that God's limitless glory thrives.

Great is our Lord and mighty in power; his understanding
has no limit.

Psalm 147:5

Dear Lord, thank you once again for Bentley. I know she
is just a dog, but you have clearly given her to me to watch
and love and learn simple lessons from. Her limitations
have not stopped her from enjoying the little joys of life.
Help me to not let mine hinder me as well. Amen.

Praise God wherever you are and whatever situation he
has allowed you to be in. His glory will shine through!

escort

-may 25, 2007

Bentley usually swims a couple of times a day in our backyard pool, but the thing is she won't swim unless I am out there with her. I'll throw the tennis ball and then she will jump in and swim and follow me as long as I am walking beside her on the banks of the pool. The funny thing is Khaki the old dog follows me too ...but she is on land! It is like it is her responsibility to escort me as I make my way to the end and back. I don't know if it is coming out of obedience or out of love; it is just funny to me. She doesn't do this occasionally but every time that Bentley swims. I will pat Khaki on the head and say good job thanks for joining me, but I can't help but wonder sometimes what she is thinking.

One thing it made me think of was that God is always walking beside me but I so often forget to take that into account. I know that Khaki is beside me. But am I that confident the God is? He has promised to never leave me or forsake me, but aren't there times when he has to take a break and attend to someone or something else? I know that answer is *no*. For he is capable and able to do all things at all times. Now really, doesn't that send some thoughts up your flagpole?

For I look at the times that I get frustrated and mess up just trying to juggle my little world. Even this morning, I was trying to juggle too many things from the refrigerator, and I knew it. I knew I had lost control, but there was not one thing I could do about it except wait to see where it was going to land. The egg hit the ground hard and cracked right open leaving a gooey mess all over the floor. When was the last time you hit the floor and crashed? Were you trying to carry too much by yourself? Was God watching then? Yes ! Could he have stopped it? Yes! But there are even lessons that I can learn over something so small and insignificant as dropping an egg.

1. Don't try to carry more than I am equipped to balance.
2. Be thankful for the food that I have.
3. Don't be in such a hurry.
4. Be grateful that I am able to bend down and clean it up.
5. Thank God that I have a family to be cooking for.

It seems like the more I pay attention to God, who is always around, the more I am able to see life as the journey instead of being so caught up in the little stuff that so often just doesn't matter. I need to continue to exercise thoughts of appreciation to God and thoughts on how to continue to simplify my comings and goings. I need to take things a little slower, and be grateful for my many blessings rather than concentrate on my many mistakes. For even the mistakes are worthy is there was some little God lesson that was learned.

God is walking beside me. Wherever I go, he is there for support, guidance, companionship and most of all he is there because he loves me. When you are around someone who truly loves you, for who you are right now with no expectation, that love gives you a freedom and safety to pursue new adventures with that *hope* that all things are going to be okay. God is that someone to each of us. How blessed we are to be called his children.

We serve an awesome God who will and does walk to the end of the pool and back just to stay beside us. Am I staying beside him? Am I showing him the same respect and courtesy through my love for him by wanting to be beside him? Or am I pushing him away and trying to run ahead? It doesn't matter if I am walking out of obedience or love …it only matters that I am walking with him.

Dear Lord, I thank you for walking beside me no matter where my feet may go. Thank you for your protection, your wisdom, and your guidance. May I be constantly aware of little lessons that you are trying to teach me even in the mundane chores of the day.

Let me not take for granted the unconditional love that you have poured into and over me. Lord, teach me to pass it on to others who may not know of your love, your grace, your mercy, and your forgiveness; forgiveness for the mistakes that sometimes rattle my insides so loudly that they block out your whispers of love. Let me be able to recognize your footprints on my heart as you walk beside me, and be ever grateful that you are my God. Amen.

Praise God wherever you are and whatever situation he has allowed you to be in. His glory will shine through!

tennis balls

-may 30, 2007

Bentley—one tennis ball was not enough. I threw it, she brought it, but the thing is she just can't let go of it. She accidentally bit my finger while I was trying to pry it from her mouth so I thought, *What happens if I throw another one? What will she do then?*

She can't stand the fact that there is a loose tennis ball, and truly, she will swim for twenty minutes straight trying to figure out how to capture both the one she has in her mouth and the one floating. One time she actually did and she had those two balls in her mouth, and it was really quite funny …but only that once. The rest of the time, she would swim in circles, nudge it with her nose, and try to push it with her mouth. I had to keep watching her because she was so intent I was afraid she would go under out of exhaustion not having enough sense to stop her pursuit.

I have felt that way, being so intent on pursuing a situation that I finally am just totally worn out from the mental anguish. (I tend to give up pretty easily if it is physical). But oh, how I can toss around and push around and nudge and swim in circles around some things. Part of it is the tendency to control; part of it is not wanting to give up when I have invested so much time and effort into trying to make it work. Maybe it is an internal "goal" thing. I want to accomplish what I have set out to do no matter if it is in my best interest or not. I sometimes think God must be sitting on his throne quite amused at the stupid quandaries I affix my energies on. So many times even if they are really of no significance, I just can't seem to shake them off. Kind of like Bentley chasing a second tennis ball.

God has taught me so many times that if I just ask for his guidance, the things on this Earth will grow strangely dim. The things that don't seem to matter to me are sometimes the greatest things that matter to him, and vice versa, some of the things that seem to really matter to me really have no eternal value or worth. Eternal value and worth. Now that might be a good measuring stick. We are on this Earth for such a short time. What are we spending that time on? What are we pursing that will last and be noted as significant in the eyes of the Lord? Probably money is not first on his list—or partying or carousing but those are some of the obvious ones. What about arguing, gossiping, trying to out do your neighbor, undermining an associate, or demanding an entitlement that you really don't deserve. Probably none of those would make it to God's "to be" list or his "to strive for" list. I am guilty of every one of those things. And then God uses the example of Bentley right in front of my eyes, and I realize that unless I am pursuing Godly goals my efforts are really in vain. I am swimming in circles accomplishing nothing, yet I am busying my mind and not leaving room for the worthy things of value.

> And this world is fading away, along with everything that people crave. But anyone who does what pleases God will live forever.
>
> 1 John 2:17

Today, think about what you are pursuing and the goals you are striving for. Maybe you don't even have any goals right now and you are just staying busy for busy sake. God has got a spot for you in his kingdom. He has got a spot for me. I just need to focus on focusing on him to let me know what it is. 'Til then maybe chasing floating tennis balls should be an option for Bentley and not for me. God has better things planned for me to do …and if I ask him what they are …he is sure to guide my way. But am I willing to give up my insignificant desires and pursue his? The true answer is sometimes *yes* and sometimes *no*. Help, Lord …I need some obedience training!

Dear Lord, I know how much time I waste chasing stupid ventures. Help me to spend my time wisely and for your good purpose. I am not saying take the fun out of living, but help me to be productive in a worthy manner. Help me to chase the ideas and desires of your heart using my talents. For I know that to be truly successful, I need to be doing what you have created me to do with the gifts that you have planted within me. Help me to recognize those gifts and not waste time swimming in circles just because I don't know what else to do. Thank you for Bentley and the continued lessons that you show me through her. Please, Lord, continue to heal her. Amen.

Praise God wherever you are and whatever situation he has allowed you to be in. His glory will shine through!

Part XII

summer play

Summer has hit and it is hot. We are spending as much time as we can in the pool and around the pool. Bentley is doing the same ole thing; swimming a little and walking a little. Ten months down the road. Can't hardly believe it has been that long when I look back. But we are in a manageable place with Bentley. And she seems comfortable in her own skin. She continues to grow and now is about 80 pounds. Her smile is as precious as ever and I am blessed by her four legged crippled presence in my life. She keeps me humble.

inside out

-june 6, 2007

We are now in the tenth month since our young lab Bentley had her accident. Doctors gave her only a five percent chance to ever walk again because of all the damage that was done to her spinal cord. Yesterday, I threw the tennis ball in the pool, and we played fetch for a few minutes …then she got out and was standing beside me then leaped on to the lounge chair. I looked at her in total disbelief and helped her down thinking that was a fluke, and I stood still for a few minutes …and she did it again! Bentley is now able to get herself up on the lounge chair by herself. What a feat!

Sometimes you never know what is going on the inside 'til it shows up on the outside. After many months of prayer for this little four-legged friend, I finally had resorted to the fact that she is just going to have a hard time from here on out. I don't know whether Bentley's new trick is a will of the mind or determined attempt of the body, but something is different and what a surprise blessing to see it right in front of my eyes.

God often works from the inside out. Sometimes there is a bunch going on in the inside before we can ever see a change on our outside. The same is true with our prayers. Even though we see no visible difference for the situation we have prayed for, that doesn't mean that God is not working behind the scenes to accomplish his mission and answer our prayers. Has there ever been someone you have prayed for over and over again, but you just don't see any results? What about a situation that seemed hopeless? Have you ever found yourself saying, "This will take an act of God to get though,!" or "Only a miracle could make this better!" or "God is going to have to be really big to conquer this habit!" Now, consider back on one of those things that *has* worked out! There have been some, I know. Did you give God the credit for it, or did you disregard the true source of the accomplishment?

Prayer is real. It is a real communication with a real God, and it is two sided. You might not hear an audible voice coming down from the heavens, but the bible tells us that God is listening and God knows our hearts and our hurts and our hallelujahs. I must say when I first started praying for Bentley to be healed, I was confident. I prayed with total trust that God would heal her in spite of the odds—almost to the point of being arrogant. Then as the months went by and Bentley continued to favor that right leg and would fall so often when she walked, I started to become discouraged and disappointed. *God has healed her so that she can get around, but this is what we have got.*

I looked back and thought, *If I had to do it over again, would I still have made the same choice? The answer is yes. For, I have learned more lessons from this little dog and the adversity that we have been through with her than I could have ever imagined. When I look in that precious face and see her gentle and happy demeanor in spite of her limitations, I see that God has answered my prayers. Not necessarily in the way I expected, but he has used even a four legged creature to bring me closer to himself because I have had to keep praying.*

This story isn't over. None of our stories are over 'til God says they are over. This is only one little example of how God works. You have seen him in your lives. You have felt his comfort, his strength, his healing, his power, and his wisdom. God is real and to achieve our Godly potential that he has orchestrated, we must stay connected to him through the lifeline that he has given us through prayer. He does answer prayers, all of them—whether they are for a four-legged friend or a war across the ocean that seemingly has no defined solution. We serve a mighty God, full of compassion who sees a whole picture in living color detail. His glory is at stake, and whether we realize it or not or accept it or not God is sitting victoriously on his throne in the Heavens. We should pray with praise and adoration to his name and give thanks for all of glorious works he has done.

When I saw Bentley leap on that chair yesterday, it reminded me to keep on praying confidently and not lose heart just because things take a while. But pray with assurance that God is listening. The prayer that we are praying sometimes isn't answered in the way in which we expect, but God is answering. He is answering in a way that will grow us up and bring us closer to a deep and significant relationship with him. He is not interested in the ways things are, as much as he is in the *way* you and I *are!* May we too take a leap of faith and trust God with our prayers with confidence, knowing that he is listening and he will answer. Be Faithful. Don't give up for you never know what God is doing on the inside that hasn't yet showed itself on the outside.

> The Lord is my strength and my shield; my heart trusts in him, and I am helped. My heart leaps for joy and I will give thanks to him in song.
>
> Psalm 28:7

Dear Lord, thank you for being in control, for remembering to change the seasons, and spin the universe and let the sun come up and the rains come down. Thank you for being the almighty God who can do anything at anytime for anybody. Let me remember, Lord, that your love is your generator, and that love is showered on me each day in ways I will never know.

When I come to you in prayer, Lord, teach me to be confident and trusting, even though I sometimes have to wait a very long time to see any glimmers of answers. Let my faith be steadfast and let your strength through your Holy Spirit be generated right on through to me. Teach me, Lord, to just take this day that is given, and live it to its fullest. I know that you hold tomorrow in your hands and it is not for me to worry over. For you are working from the inside out, and today's seeds will be tomorrow's flowers. Let us leap, Lord, right into your loving arms with our prayers, and trust you to answer them your way. Amen.

Praise God wherever you are and whatever situation he has allowed you to be in. His glory will shine through!

hope

-june 27, 2007

Bentley stands at my back door, quietly, just looking in in hopes that I will notice her and bring her some left over breakfast. She knows it is possible because it has been done before. She waits, watches, and hopes. Then after a while, she gives up realizing things have moved on, and she heads on to her bed. She is at the mercy of her caretaker.

We too are at the mercy of our caretaker. We stand at his door waiting and watching and hoping for we have seen his miracles, we have witnessed his hand upon this situation, and we know his potential, but what are his plans for this one. We must continue to believe in God's goodness even if all things are telling us not too. He might not react in a manner that is timely in our scope, but he will react, and he will answer your prayers.

We broke up into small groups in Sunday school at CEPC, and Roger Wernette, our teacher, is trying desperately to get us to disciple one another. So after his lesson, he left time for us to team up and talk about his appointed questions. The basis for the questions Sunday was the story of Jesus in the boat with his disciples when a storm became so furious. The waters were raging and Jesus was sleeping and the disciples were desperately and fearfully trying to secure the boat, but Jesus continued to sleep. Finally, energy spent, they woke him.

These were the questions that Roger put together for our small group discussions, some pretty good ones to ponder .

1. If you were one of the disciples, what would you have wanted Jesus to do during and about the storm? Think beyond, "Just stop the storm."
2. How have you felt during the storms of life? What did you want most? What would be better to desire? What do you think that you need to be learning right now about Jesus? How are you learning that? Are your current storms, fears, or anxieties (be they major or minor) teaching you?
3. What is the key question(s) that we need to ask when the storms hit?
4. How do you think modern day Christians are doing in their thinking and actions to accurately reflect the true essence of the Christian life? What helps or distracts them as they go through life?

The main one that I want to key on is the third one? When this cancer deal hit our lives with Molly, our sixteen-year-old, I remember thinking, *I don't even know how to pray?* Of course, I would pray for healing, wisdom, and comfort but what do I ask God for after that? Then I just started telling God everything that was on my mind, and I even interjected a few *where did this come from comments, why*

Molly and not me? and all the usual insecurities. Am I strong enough to handle this? Is she? Will she be healed? When?

When we were discussing these questions, my friend Charlie said, "We are all so familiar with the verse from Romans that says all things work together for good (Romans 8:28)." But he said, "The real verses that we need to lean on are the verses right before them." (Romans 8:26–27) In the same way, the Spirit helps us in our weakness. We do not know what we ought to pray for, but the Spirit himself intercedes for us with groans that words cannot express. And he who searches our hearts knows the mind of the Spirit, because the Spirit intercedes for the saints in accordance with God's will.

I've read and reread these verses this week and have continued to keep them on my mind ever since Sunday, for what a true base for security and contentment in knowing that we don't have to get it right when we pray. We only have to pray, and the Holy Spirit will translate those thoughts and words right to the throne room of God.

Haven't you sometimes wondered why things have turned out the way that they did? This is not what you or I prayed for. Our hope has to come from the fact that we know we have been heard, not that we already know the answer, but that there will be an answer to a request that has been translated on our behalf. It won't necessarily be the answer we are expecting because the request we have made might have been altered in the intercession, God knowing what it is that we really need.

When Prayers Don't Seem To Be Answered

I asked God to take away my pain.

God said, No. It is not for me to take away, but for you to give it up.

I asked God to make my handicapped child whole.

God said, No. Her spirit was whole, her body was only temporary.

I asked God to grant me patience.

God said, No. Patience is a byproduct of tribulations; it isn't granted, it is earned.

I asked God to give me happiness.

God said, No. I give you blessings. Happiness is up to you.

I asked God to spare me pain.

God said, No. Suffering draws you apart from worldly cares and brings you closer to me.

I asked God to make my spirit grow.

God said, No. You must grow on your own, but I will prune you to make you fruitful.

I asked for all things that I might enjoy life.

God said, No. I will give you life so that you may enjoy all things.

I ask God to help me LOVE others, as much as he loves me.

God said …Ahhhh, finally you have the idea.

Author unknown

Just like Bentley, we too are at the mercy of our caretaker he provides for our needs and gives us treats sometimes when we expect it and so many sometimes when we don't. But we must always hold on to the hope that God is just on the other side of the door, and his bounties are without measure and beyond compare. He has shown us his good deeds of the past, and we know that he will continue to bless us in every way if stay close beside him and wait upon his timing! His blessings might sometimes be disguised ...but they will always be something that grows us up or bring us closer to him ...and that is the greatest blessing of all.

Dear Lord, thank you for sending us an intercessor who acts according to our best interest and your best purposes.

Praise God wherever you are and whatever situation he has allowed you to be in. His glory will shine through!

good deeds
-june 28, 2007

In a familiar quote by Clare Boothe Luce it is said that, "No good deed goes unpunished,"[8] and today when I let Bentley in the house, I was reminded of that. For I just thought the dogs would like to hang out in the kitchen while I was making breakfast, and not two minutes later Bentley made a mistake on the floor. It was my fault, I knew I should have taken them out on the grass before letting them in, especially Bentley because she still gets so "puppy excited." But the good deed even if it was for the dogs did backfire. When a good deed is done, we do usually expect some sort of recognition it is just human nature to want someone to notice. Around my house, I don't wait for them to notice. I point it out, and by now, my group has figured out to say the appropriate response, "Great job, Mom!" or "Looking great, Mom!" And then they are welcome to go about their business. I just want them to notice when I do something on their account.

God are you watching? Did you see? Did you hear? Oswald Chambers made me mindful of how putting the emphasis on me and my deeds is taking the emphasis off of him and his deeds. If I truly am serving God as I should and as I aspire to, I really don't have time to be looking for approval or appreciation from others because I should be so busy and so voluntarily submitted to God through my thoughts and behavior that anything other than God would reap unproductive and fleeting benefits.

On June 27 in *My Utmost for His Highest,* he states:

"The Sermon on the Mount indicates that when we are on a mission for Jesus Christ, there is no time to stand up for ourselves. Jesus says, in effect, "'Don't worry about whether or not you are being treated justly.'"" Looking for justice (or in my case accolades) is actually a sign that we have been diverted from our devotion to him. "Never look for justice in the world but never cease to give it. If we look for justice, we will only begin to complain and to indulge ourselves in the discontent of self-pity, as if to say, "'Why should I be treated like this?'" Continue steadily on with what I have told you to do, and I will guard your life. If you try to guard it yourself, you remove yourself from my deliverance. We put our common sense on the throne and then attach God's name to it."[9]

In essence it goes back to everything is about God. I have to stay steady, stay focused and do what I know is in God's will. If by chance I get confused as to what God's will is or what my will is, I have to ask"am I after accolades for God or for me?" Maybe I need to back off a little on requiring my family to notice my good deeds., and expecting verbal rewards. Oswald is right: if I indulge in self and do things only for response of others then complaining and self pity do take a seat on the throne, and it is not my throne. So many times we do lean to our own understanding, instead of trusting God with all our hearts (see Proverbs 3:3–5)."

> In the same way, good deeds are obvious, and even those that are not cannot be hidden.
>
> 1 Timothy 5:25

There will be many chances to try this out. God generally sends something my way the very day I write something like this. I hope that maybe I will consider my deeds and chores and do them without expectation of someone noticing, but rather with private contentment that God is watching. As long as I have him in focus the deeds will be stamped with his recognition. "No good deed goes unpunished." Maybe so, but good deeds do make their mark even if they are rejected or stomped on or acknowledged or not. They count! Don't be discouraged into thinking that all is being done for naught. Let your heart be rewarded by just knowing that you have done a right or honorable or good thing and don't let Satan get in there and tell you otherwise. And even if no one else notices …God is noticing …and as long as we are doing unto him because of him …and through him……. it counts! No matter how big or small the deed may be. *It counts!*

Dear Lord, we do lean on our own understanding and often times don't regard your presence in our big picture.

Let us do your good through our lives and be content with your stamp of recognition and not rely on the approval of man. Amen.

Praise God wherever you are and whatever situation he has allowed you to be in. His glory will shine through!

distraction

-july 18, 2007

Bentley just loves playing fetch in the swimming pool, and she stays focused on the ball whether it is in hand or in the pool. But there is one distraction that causes her to forfeit all attention of the game at hand—George, the cat. Bentley is so intrigued by the cautious, deliberate walk, the low-slivered intensity that George shows when he is casing out a situation and Bentley can't understand why when everyone else pays attention to her that George remains aloof. So she drops her ball from her mouth and hurries to the door where George is meowing to get in and greets him with hopes that maybe this time he will be attentive to her. It doesn't happen. George is much too independent, and finally, after sniffing and watching for several minutes with no response, Bentley loses interest and returns to the tennis ball.

What is it that intrigues me and causes me to lose focus and get off path? It doesn't necessarily have to be a right or wrong issue. Just something that that seems to pull me towards a desire to tap into that which I just don't seem to be able to get my arms around. Maybe it is curiosity, maybe just looking for a new flare for life, or maybe it is something that I know is wrong but the lure is too great to dismiss it. This game between George and Bentley is not new. George clearly knows he is being coy and cool, and Bentley clearly gets sucked into his web of torment and tease each time that cat appears. I too must be careful and approach the unknown with a cautious bit of timidity. Because sometimes the very things that entice me are the ones that will end up trapping me if I get too close.

There are things in my life right now that I am asking God to pull me away from …because the unseen forces of luring temptation seem to whittle away at my stronghold. One of those temptations is this computer. I seem to have become, as my daughter Jennifer would say, a computer junkie. A little of this captivating machine goes a long way and so many times I find that I can waste away several, what could have been very productive hours, by trying to figure out how to manipulate some of its features or cruising sites of interest. I need some serious discipline and a stronghold to pull me away and direct me to more substantial and relative real life interests that have merit.

Maybe with you it might not be a computer, maybe it's a habit of another sort or a pull that has different effects, but I know some of you know what I mean. You just get sucked in to something, and before you know it, it has got you, and the undertow is too powerful for us to get out of it alone. We need someone with a strong hold.

How strong is your stronghold? I have to ask myself that so many times? And who is my stronghold? Or what is it? A stronghold is something or someone that has a strong hold on you. *Where* are you going to get help? Or *who* are you going to ask for help or who are you depending on to establish a baseline for the stronghold in you life? The world offers us a bunch of choices. There are a bunch of luring temptations whining at the door to get in, but do I want to subject myself to what appears to be an innocent temptation? Am I willing to be sidetracked by a whining distraction that is adding nothing to my life but frustration, torment, or temporary satisfaction? Certainly not, but when the intrigue is in my face, it is a pretty illusive force to contend with.

He is my loving God and my fortress, my stronghold and my deliverer, my shield, in whom I take refuge, who subdues peoples under me.

Psalm 144:2

There is only one stronghold powerful enough to battle the "Georges" in our lives who entice us at every turn through their coy seduction of more, more, more, or striving to get you to settle for good when best is just a reach away - it is God! Clearly and simply God. He is the one you can count on to give your courage when you are weak at the knees, strength to make a stand when all others around you are stumbling, to help you find calm in the midst of a storm, peace when the fires around you are blazing with unrest, or a hand when you feel like you are sinking.

Who is whining at your door trying like crazy for you to let them in? Just ask God, if he would, to please answer the door, he'll quiet the noises, send them away, and you will once again be at peace.

Dear Lord, temptations pull and tug at me from all angles, and you know what my weaknesses are and what my needs are. So many times the temptations that are so effective are the very ones that seem to fill one of my needs, and that is why they are so effective. Help me to look to you for my needs and not be satisfied with temporary quick fixes that are not only insufficient but cause me to falter in the long run. Be my stronghold. Remind me to come to you and ask you to be the strong one that I hold on to. And if I am not paying attention and get pulled under by the forces, please, Lord, hold strong to me and pull me from the grasp of unhealthy and unworthy life grabbers. Amen.

Praise God wherever you are and whatever situation he has allowed you to be in. His glory will shine through!

clicker
-July 19, 2007

There is a dog training technique that was suggested to me by one of Bentley's vets to use on Bentley to encourage her to stay up and walk. It is called clicker training. Just as it sounds, you have a clicker, and each time the dog does what is asked of him or her, you click it. It is an approval based technique. This was mentioned to me in January, and I discounted it because the use of a clicker I thought would make me crazy ...click, click, click! Then last week I was reading an article in *Good Housekeeping,* and it too talked about the success of clicker training. It brought this up to the front of my mind again. I thought, *If a consistent click represents success or achievement and praise ...then why wouldn't a consistent word of praise do the same thing?* So I started trying it on Bentley. Every time she started running (or hopping as she often does) with her back legs instead of dragging, I would praise her. I would praise her when she would walk and stay up; I would praise her when she would come when called. I made an effort to watch for times to praise her. And she did respond to it. At first, I thought, *I just want this to work so I am thinking that it is working.* But tonight I realistically evaluated it, and I think it truly does make a difference.

Encouragement through kind words and words of praise have a significant power on those they are spoken to.

They bring hope and provide a sense of accomplishment, appreciation, and acknowledgment to the heart of one who hears it. I think of the times when someone has told me that I have done a good job. It makes me want to do better or at least maintain a healthy status of approval. Bentley is no different. I think we all tend to gravitate towards praise whether we acknowledge it or not. It feels good when someone speaks up and says something nice about something that we have accomplished.

There is such power in words. Words of encouragement can motivate and lift and raise the spirits of someone almost immediately. And conversely, words of complaint and frustration and attack can discourage one just as quickly. (There is some well known formula about the effect of how many positive comments it takes to negate one negative comment and why positive comments can be such a motivational tool.) I know we don't live in a "Pollyanna" world, but the spoken word is a mighty tool that has the power to encourage and lighten and brighten the very soul of someone you love or someone who has just brushed across your path. It takes a little effort, and you have to train yourself to notice the times when a praise could be extended , but what a difference it makes. Click out an encouragement then click out another one.

Your love has given me great joy and encouragement, because you, brother, have refreshed the hearts of the saints.

Philemon 1:7

(I love the word refreshed for that is such a reaction to encouragement. It refreshes your soul like cool water on a hot afternoon.) Looking for the good in someone else helps you to focus on the good in you too because, just like Bentley, when she responds to the praise that I have given her and reacts to a way that is being taught, success is not only hers but mine as well. What if we had a tape rolling inside our heads of the voice of God praising us when we choose to obey or respond to his command in a timely manner or stepped out of our comfort zone and pursued someone or something in a way that would give him glory. We would be walking around on air, filled with delight that we had done the right thing and pleased the very God who had made us.

We all know right from wrong, so does Bentley, but it is our choice as to how we are going to react. Sometimes that very word of encouragement or praise is what keeps us on tract and makes us strive to keep on going in the right direction. As I catch Bentley responding in a way that is healthy and good, I praise her. So is our Father above watching as we go about our lives, and he too is praising our choices when they are in step with his will for us.

Dear Lord, may we be conscious of praising others who are before us. Let us look for ways to encourage one another through the spoken word and bring glory to you in the way we lift others up. It sometimes is a challenge, Lord, to find the good but if we look through your loving eyes on those who have been put in our path, we too will find that there is potential for success in each of us. May the praise that we give be genuine and may it edify the one who it is given to. For the good that is within us or the good that we do is a reflection of your indwelling spirit within us.

Praise God wherever you are and whatever situation he has allowed you to be in. His glory will shine through!

rhythm

-july 11, 2007

Things remain pretty much the same with my little four legged lab friend, Bentley. She still has a tough time walking with that weak back leg, but I keep thinking, *She has beat the odds.* I have found that because her one back leg is so weak that she puts a log of emphasis on the other one to compensate, thus the nails on the other one need protection as well. So I bought her some new shoes, again, and she just seems to go along with the flow and accepts them. I walk them (she and Khaki) each night in the front yard but to get to the front we have to go down the back driveway.

I would always watch Bentley to make sure she wasn't dragging. It is the lazy way out for her and certainly not good for the rest of her body. *But with the shoes,* I don't have to watch any more. I merely have to listen for the rhythm of her stride, and when I hear the shoes hit the concrete, I know she is *up.*

There is a rhythm to our stride as well. As long as things are going unshaken we remain up, but when we get tired or submit to laziness, we have a tendency to try to slide by. God recognizes the rhythm, and that is when he stops us and gently says, "Get up you can do it. You just have to put on my shoes of protection and tackle the concrete hard things that are before you." We need to walk in the shoes of strength and courage and wisdom and not go dragging around just because it is an easier way of dealing with the problem.

If we don't use the muscles we've got then they grow weak. We've got muscles; God's muscles. We are able to stand tall in the shadows of adversity because God is Bigger than the adversity. He is standing with us, willing, so willing to be our comfort and to be our shoes of protection. Life can hit pretty hard just like that concrete and seemly have no give. When we go out bare footed with tender souls, we can't help but be subjected to pain that sometimes seems unbearable. We need the protection that God gives. He knows when our rhythm is off, and he is right there to help us up. *Right there beside you.* Tender souls we are, and we need protection.

"I am the LORD, the God of all mankind. Is anything too hard for me?"

Jeremiah 32:27

My rhythm was off yesterday after Molly and I went to TCH for follow up tests. We had been home only a few hours when they called and said we didn't get all the images we needed to have a concise report. We have made an appointment for you to come back tomorrow. My protective shoes went on immediately, and I said, "*No,* we are not coming back. We have just spent most of the morning and part of the afternoon there and just because someone else made a mistake doesn't mean that my child will have to bear the consequences." I was totally out of sorts and frustrated and talking about being off rhythm. I was wobbling on hard concrete with no protection.

There was nothing that indicated any unusual results in the pictures that they had taken, so I told them we would talk again at the end of August. She had full day summer school classes for the next three weeks, and we just weren't going to push this button again so soon— especially if there was no evidence that it was needed. God was watching and part of me knows that he knows how the motherly protection works, but part of me also knows that the frustration in my voice to the supervisor could have been softened and I could have been more understanding that mistakes do happen, and a little more grace could and would have accomplished the same results.

And then when Mel came home he said, "We have to be grateful that she is in remission and look at the big picture." He is so right. I so often times get caught in the little stuff and forget to look at the big picture. Do you see why God is having me write these devotionals? I still don't get it so much of the time! And if I do get it I'm often times not using what I've got! A work in progress I am …thank God he is patient and deliberate in teaching his lessons day by day and step by step I know he is changing me because he knows I want to get it right. I just need a great deal more practice.

We get rattled, sure, and want to use our own strength and quickly move along bare footed, but what I must remember is: to do whatever I do or say whatever I say ... wearing God's shoes. I must take time to put them on, for my tender-soled shoes are merely light weight slippers and are not durable. And they surely don't have the protection that his do. When I am wearing God's shoes, it doesn't matter how hard the surface or how long the walk ...I am protected. God is listening to my rhythm, and he knows when I am down. And he stands quietly by my side and encourages me to get on back up! You can do it. You can too!

Dear Lord, just keep on sending me the same lessons and keep trying to teach them using different lesson plans. One day I might be able to get it and keep it and use what I have gotten. Thank you for being patient. Amen

Praise God wherever you are and whatever situation he has allowed you to be in. His glory will shine through!

leashed
-august 6, 2007

They had to be boarded for the first time. Khaki and Bentley have never been away from this house without us, but this was the wedding weekend for my son, and I just wasn't okay with Bentley not having someone around all the time. I picked the dogs up on Sunday afternoon when we got back to town. They had both been washed, but Bentley was different after only three days. Her sores looked better; she was walking better, standing straighter, and, of course, smelled great after her bath! What had they done? First of all, I figured out that most of the dogs that are kenneled are healthy dogs not needing too much extra care.

Just as it is when we go to the park, when people see Bentley, if they are animal lovers, they are immediately empathetic towards her and want to know what happened. The folks at Urban Tails had the history and they knew her story, and there was one lady, who had a true heart for a handicapped dog, and she was Bentley's friend for the weekend. When I asked what she had done she said, "I put aloe Vera on her wounds each day, I walked her alone with a leash, I waited when she fell down for her to get herself back up, and I took off her shoe, and every once in a while, I would scratch her under the neck because she just loved that. I trusted a stranger with my little four-legged friend, and I was blessed by the loving care that was extended to her. I took her on a walk that night using the leash and leaving off the shoe. The difference was amazing. I want her to have the freedom to explore and smell, so I always let the dogs free in the yard. I found that Bentley doesn't necessarily need that freedom. For we walked a lot further with the leash, and she fell less often because she was forced to slow down.

I don't know about you all, but I want my freedom. I want to be free to explore and seek adventure on my own timing, but just because that is what I want to do, it is not necessarily what is the best thing for me to do.

I have found that to be true repeatedly. I need a leash to hold me back and slow me down sometimes. And it is not only the freedom "to do" but the freedom "to say" and often times "to boss". For example, I have a tendency to think that I need to be involved in so many of the decision making processes of those around me. This weekend I realized that I need to back off and give other people (especially my precious family) an opportunity to get a job done without interfering. It is hard for me to believe, but they really don't need my input. And often times, I say too much and push too hard and get going too fast. Gosh, I hate admitting that, but it's true.

We all need boundaries. Freedom is great but freedom within God's boundaries is what is truly liberating. I have found that when I am open to instruction and take time to pay attention to what I am doing or what I am saying, I tend to not get so wound up. Instead of just reacting, I take a little time to think it through, and it goes better for everybody.

Bentley was happy just to have me by her side on a walk. She was not concerned that she didn't have the freedom to take her own route or slide into a new scent. She was proud to be up and walking. For several days, she has followed a new routine by a new person, and it had paid off. I have allowed Bentley to follow the same pattern, thinking this is what we've got! But it took someone who was not familiar with her routine and who loved her enough to be patient with her, make her walk slow, cautious enough to not trust her without a leash, and dedicated enough to stay with her in spite of her handicap. Thank God we are not what "we have got". For each day with God's help we will see new things and think new thoughts and follow new paths. I needed a new look on Bentley.

> He has showed you, O man, what is good. And what does the LORD require of you? To act justly and to love mercy and to walk humbly with your God.
>
> Micah 6:8

I know someone who is just the same with me, as this new person was with Bentley. God. For God loves me enough to slow me down when I am going too fast, helps me to recognize his leash to direct me and pace me, and is dedicated to stay beside me and with me in spite of my many handicaps. Bentley was at the mercy of a newfound friend, and it was to her definite advantage.

If I too would chose to be at the mercy of God, I know I would see improvements in my life as well. For his designated routine for my ways, my thoughts, my words, and my deeds requires that I do have boundaries. And it is through those boundaries that I will continue to learn to be more in step with his pace. Freedom is sweeter if it is freedom that is within the limits of God. For if we have freedom without God's boundaries, we so often find ourselves floundering or dragging in a hurried state just to get the job done, and we miss the satisfaction of true enjoyment and accomplishment. God's leash just helps us to look better, walk better, and stand up straighter, and we will even smell better because we will have been bathed with his glory.

Dear Lord, thank you that you continually are showing me ways to undo some of my old habits. Let me be willing to listen and then willing to act on what I know you have shown to me. Let me not struggle to shake off the leash of your way but be content in the boundaries that you have given me. Remind me that I don't have to be involved in all the decisions around me. For you have given others a keen sense of responsibility and purpose and often times when I interfere I am not allowing them the joy of accomplishing their purpose or using their gifts. I also was reminded, Lord, this weekend that others sometimes have new working ideas that really work. Let me be open to new ways of doing things and not be stuck in old habits that are not beneficial. Amen.

Praise God wherever you are and whatever situation he has allowed you to be in. His glory will shine through!

Part XIII

about the same

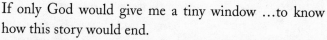

If only God would give me a tiny window ...to know how this story would end.

But that is not God's style. It has been a year, and we have done the best that we could have done to care for this precious dog. Though I continue to pray for her complete healing, I must be content with the prayers thus far that God has answered. For through this journey, I have learned that God cares about what we care about. Either he cares and is willing to help us continue what we have started, or he cares enough to help us change tracks. For right now with Bentley, apparently God is helping us to stay on this track ...and keep on going one day at a time, one prayer at a time, one answer at a time.

suffering
-september 6, 2007

It has been a year now since her accident …and Bentley, my four-legged friend is about the same. The "Raising Bentley" book is stewing on the back burner, and one day I hope to see that one, too, in print. I bring this story up because many of you have asked and have a true heart for animals but also as a reminder that sometimes what we pray for, in this instance for complete healing for Bentley, God answers in a different way than we have requested. Remember that saying that says, "Sometimes God calms the storm and sometimes God lets the storm rage and calms the child." I think that is the way it is with healing. Sometimes God chooses to heal the inflicted and sometimes God uses the inflicted to heal us. For through the suffering of another, we often are forced to realize the blessings that we have in our own hand.

There are no answers to *why* when we are watching and praying for another who is in such pain or discomfort. It is so often an emotional wipe out and reinstates the fact that we truly are so helpless in regard to life's outcomes. We can make choices, but God's *say* in the end is what matters and what stands. For we serve a mighty God, and just because things don't go as we have prayed, God is still God. He hasn't and doesn't and won't change. His plans and his ways are perfect though we so many times can't seem to understand them or embrace them. There will be suffering, Christ especially showed us that. And there will be hardships, but as long as we stay focused on God and not the circumstances, he will help us to find a positive outlook. Beth, a bible study friend replied to an e-mail I sent earlier in the week about two little girls frolicking in the rain as Dad held an umbrella and watched. She said there are always different ways to look at the same situation. You just have to be mindful to do it. Beth shared a story of her friend who had colon cancer, and this friend who is in the middle of true adversity seemed to always be able to find the splash in the wake of the rain. Things can be just horrible, and we can be feeling as lowly as a worm, but God has the power and the might to help us stand up and keep moving forward. In his book *Why a Suffering World Makes Sense*, Chris Teagreen writes:

"God's glory doesn't fade. It's eternal. The honor we bring to him in the crucible of life will stand as a trophy forever. The character he reveals to us in our deepest trials will give us glimpses of the unfathomable Almighty that many earthbound creatures will perhaps never see. Though the pain of this world is agonizing and devastating, the costs of experiencing it can never outweigh the benefits of the glory he reveals about himself or the glory of the character he develops in us. We get a strong sense in the Bible that if we saw the end result, we would tolerate much more the means of displaying it. Why? Because we, by the work of God in our hearts, become partakers of his glory. He shares it with us." [10]

> Now if we are children, then we are heirs—heirs of God and co-heirs with Christ, if indeed we share in his sufferings in order that we may also share in his glory.
>
> Romans 8:17

Bentley is crippled and handicapped no doubt, but only in her body. Her spirit and her attitude are just as God would have it—glad to be alive! Her insufficiencies are just little blemishes compared to her love for life and the people she loves and who love her back! You see what I mean about what God *teaches* me through *watching* her! May I be as loving and forgiving and accepting as my Bentley. She sees only the good through her conditional circumstances, and it wasn't by training that she got there, it came from within! So what lies within me? or Who lies within me?

Dear Lord, there is suffering around me and about me. I see it everyday in small ways and big. I get frustrated that I can't fix it …especially when it is someone I dearly love! But Lord, let me let them work through it, for I know that my character is being molded by watching. But I also know that their character is too being transformed through your glory. Help me, Lord, to maintain a positive attitude in spite of illness or suffering or circumstances. Let my appreciation for the blessings you have given me be a reflection back to you of the love I have for you, who you are, and all that you have done, are doing, and will do in my days to come. Let my suffering be wrapped with hope, one that is an eternal and everlasting *hope!* Amen.

Praise God wherever you are and whatever situation he has allowed you to be in. His glory will shine through!

doubt
-october 5, 2007

I watch her carefully, evaluating her gait, looking carefully at the muscles as she moves her legs, wondering, *Is she better or not? Is there really any change or am I just wishing so hard that there was that I start conjuring improvement up in my mind?* It has been a year now. Bentley *is* walking, a little uncoordinated, but she is on all fours, and she even runs hopping in unison with her back two. People do stop and stare and often ask what happened to her? Which makes me think that maybe God is using her as a vessel because I always can say, "She only had a five percent chance to walk again, and through prayer, look what she is able to do."

If you were to look at her face, she is one smiling and happy dog, and her spirit is unaffected by her handicap. I tell you this story because it occurred to me this week when I was reading *The Battle is the Lord's* by Tony Evans that I had prayed for her recovery and still do, but I have to say it hasn't been with full fledged faith. I wasn't sure she was going to walk again. There was always that little seed of doubt, and the question of: did we do the right thing? When Tony Evans talks of Eve's dilemma, what was the one thing that Satan used as his grandest tool to unsettle Eve and to scramble her thoughts? It was that God might not be so good after all? Why would he not

want you to eat from that particular tree? It was doubt!
Per Evans, "Satan came at Eve with a subtle attack that
cast doubt on the authority of God's word."[II]

> Now the serpent was more crafty than any of the wild
> animals the LORD God had made. He said to the
> woman, "did God *really* say: you must not eat from *any*
> tree in the garden?"
>
> Genesis 3:1

Doubt! Oh, how I think we underestimate the authority
of God, the power of God, and the sovereignty of God.
We go about our business taking all of those realities for
granted. Then when something big comes up, don't you
sometimes question God's ability to conquer it? Bentley
is my example here. Do I really believe that God is able to
heal Bentley to where she can walk easily and without a
struggle. Yes, I do believe that, but then I have to ask, "Do
I have faith that he will?" I doubt it! That little sprinkle
of doubt is Satan's tool to keep me from accepting God's
call for Bentley. No different than Eve. That little nudge
of doubt. When Satan asked, "Did God really say, 'you
must not eat from any tree in the garden?'" (Genesis 3:1).
It is questioning the authority of God and the validity of
God's boundaries. You see, to me, I am called to not only
erase that doubt but to guard against it springing up in
the first place. It is not my call whether or not Bentley
is healed fully. I have asked for it, but it is God's call as

to whether or not he is going to do it. God's boundaries and his reasons are all a part of his plan. And whatever his call, it should not matter. For whatever the situation God has decided upon, his glory will shine through, and his lessons will be there for me to discern consciously and unconsciously.

Doubt.
"D"evisive
"O"pportunities
"U"sed
"B"y the
"T"empter

Satan wants to divide us from God, and whatever doubt he can muster up and use for his success, he will certainly find it and use it for his warped glory and his satisfaction. To doubt God and his authority is to stand on the other side of faith. Faith is believing with all your heart that God sees the struggle and has a plan to get you through it. But that does not always mean that he will take the struggle away. Not that he can't, because he can, but that he won't. For God's glory is sometimes tucked away in the struggle and it is for us to discover.

I look at Bentley and am reminded of the many lessons God has taught me through caring for her. Lessons of devotion, discipline, how to ask for help (that is a hard one for me), how to be patient and most of all how to be thankful; for she is walking again, and her tail is even wagging again, (in a very unconventional way). I have learned how to be appreciative; for that little dog appreciates every moment of loving kindness that is extended. Do I? And I have learned that a leash isn't a bad thing. It helps keep me from going too fast and wandering in places of danger. I pray that God will help me to come to understand the impact and its true meaning of the following verse, and believe the words fully with my heart and mind. Because if I do, I will forever be shielded from the "doubt" factor that Satan uses so intently for my demise.

> Jesus replied, "I tell you the truth, if you have faith and do not doubt, not only can you do what was done to the fig tree, but also you can say to this mountain, 'Go, throw yourself into the sea,' and it will be done.'"
>
> Matthew 21:21

What are you praying for? God is able to do more than we ask more than we can imagine so reach for the stars - for the impossible.

> Now to him who is able to do immeasurably more than all we ask or imagine, according to his power that is at work within us, to him be glory.
>
> Ephesians 3:19

God hears our prayers. Have faith. His power is at work within us at this very moment. He *is able* to do immeasurably more than we ask so we must remember to ask with a faithful heart and ask without limitations. I know that doubt has crept into many of your lives as well; beware of the author of lies and the one of despicable character. Cast your doubts to the sea and stand firm on truth, for we serve a mighty and *honest* and loving God. Don't let Satan come clutter up your heart with his deception. Simply trust God to be who he says he is and do what he says he will do …for he answers our prayers and promises to never ever leave us stranded and alone.

As far as Bentley goes, God is able to heal her completely, and today I am asking with a different focus. You are able, Lord, to do this. I ask because you are able …I trust because you are sovereign. I will continue to *faithfully* pray for Bentley's healing and will no longer let doubt be an element of the prayer; for that only lessens the credit I give to God. I will pray with thanksgiving and a renewed confidence that things are going just as God has planned. I am convinced that he faithfully answers my prayers but I must remember the answers are through his eyes though not mine.

Dear Lord, doubt can and does work on emotions and play mind games and has the ability to unsettle any situation. It is a toy in the playground where Satan plays. Please keep us protected from his schemes! Amen.

Praise God wherever you are and whatever situation he has allowed you to be in. His glory will shine through!

catch up
-october 23, 2007

Sometimes you just need a new look at an old deal. I took the dogs out late the other night and asked Mel if he wanted to come along. He did and had new eyes to an old situation—*walking the dogs*. It had been a while since he had seen Bentley on a walk. Khaki was free to roam because she minds so well, and Bentley was on a leash. Mel suggested that next time maybe they should both be on a least and then Bentley wouldn't be so inclined to be chasing Khaki to get first scent. It was a terrific observation, which I am sure has been suggested to me on other occasions but I am a slow learner, Even if I did try it once, I am so inconsistent that it was quickly aborted for something easier. It worked. Khaki seemed just fine to be on a leash, and Bentley really did the best job walking that she has done in a while. She took it slow and the stumbling was not so apparent. The reason? She had nothing to chase, and no one to race.

So who are we chasing? Who are we racing? There always seems to be someone we are following or someone we aspire to be like, and our pick isn't always for the best of reasons. We tend to wish for a bigger house or a second house, for a better job, for a cuter look, for more money, for grandchildren, for someone else's lifestyle, for freedom from responsibility, to be a better golfer, for a better friend, a better spouse. We even vie for a better spot in the parking lot.

The more we chase, the more we stumble into frustration because the focus changes from doing what we are able to do …to trying to accomplish what someone else is doing. The chase is on and then we tend to lose our balance. There will always be something or someone on our want list. There will always be someone more successful, someone with more savvy, someone with greater abilities, someone with more stuff.

I talked to my sister the other day, and she was sharing a thought of a sermon she heard last week. It was about being comfortable under your own umbrella. We are all pretty good at something, but it is when we start trying to mimic someone else or compare what we have to what others have that we get into a frustrated mode of trying to keep up and step up.

If we strive to be the best at what we do, whatever we do, without worrying about what the next person is doing, then contentment will be the end result. It is hard sometimes to look at circumstances and see how different they all are and wonder why some things happen to some people while others seem to coast through without the hardships and heartaches.

The truth be known …we all have hardships and heartaches. Some are just able to hide them and suppress them better than others. Some hardships are for the world to see, and there is no way to tuck them away. Then there are other tough things tucked away in the depths of our hearts that we live with and through each day. We are dealt what we've got, but whatever we have, has gone first through the fingers of God himself. We are called to do the best with what we've been blessed with.

We are called to walk with contentment down the tough roads as well as the smooth surfaced ones. Contentment is figuring out how to be happy with what you have, and what we have is a God who loves us with all his heart. He is there to walk beside us. He is there to walk behind us, he is there to walk before us, He knows our speed. We don't have to be walking fast and running to catch up with him. As a matter of fact God is usually a fairly slow and methodical mover. To maintain his speed, we probably need to slow down and stop the racing and the chasing. Help me to stay focused on my own pace and not try to run someone else's race.

I know what it is to be in need, and I know what it is to have plenty. I have learned the secret of being content in any and every situation, whether well fed or hungry, whether living in plenty or in want.

Philippians 4:12

Bentley needed an older and wiser counterpart to walk beside her, and once she was side by side with her friend, she was able to settle down and enjoy the walk. Maybe if I would slow down and pay attention to God, my older and wiser counselor, who has offered to come along side me …then I too would have a more enjoyable walk of life.

For he knows my pace, and he also knows there are plenty of blessings for all of us. We need not run, thinking we will miss what he has in store. If God has designated the blessing for me then it will be there when I get there and I don't have to compete to receive it. To him be the Glory for walking me through my story.

Dear Lord, I do need to take time and walk slower and not be chasing errands and deadlines and people whose lives are so different from mine. Let me fare with contentment the blessings that have been so graciously sent my way. I know some of the things I see don't always look like blessings, but I also know that you can and will use them all to mold me into the person you have called me to be. Let me look at circumstances that surround me and search for the best in them. For there is nothing that comes my way that has not first been allowed by you, and if you have brought me to it, you will also bring me through it. Amen.

Praise God wherever you are and whatever situation he has allowed you to be in. His glory will shine through!

understand

-october 28, 2007

Why had I not fed them at the usual seven o'clock? Why did I let them sleep inside? Why did I try to give Bentley a bath in the utility room sink? (That had to be a pretty funny sight. But what was I thinking?) Why did we go for a walk so early? Why did Bentley get to go in the car and Khaki have to stay in the kitchen? I am not too sure how much dogs can understand and question ...but one thing I know is that Bentley was confused. She didn't understand why the routine was different?

She was going to be spayed this morning, and she wasn't allowed any food after 10:00 p.m. She has a bladder infection, and I was trying to be thoughtful to the doctor, as far as the walk and a little bathroom time, as well as a little fun before we left! I knew the plan. Bentley didn't understand, and there was no way to help her see the whole picture. She just was going to have to trust me. She knows how much I love her. She stays close by and tries to obey everything I ask her to do, and even though she didn't understand, she followed my requests.

We don't see God's whole picture either. We don't understand why things happen as they do and we are not able to imagine the detailed workings of God's plan. We just have to trust that God will lead us to the place he wants us to be, guide us to do the things he wants us to do and mold us through these experiences to be who he wants us to be! God has his reasons for allowing things that we don't understand to happen. Sometimes we get a glimpse of the reasons sometimes we don't. Bentley needed to be spayed; her little body couldn't go through a pregnancy, and even if it could, she would have a hard time being a mom and getting around with puppies. We had to make that decision on her behalf because we are responsible for her well-being.

There are times when God detours our lives as well, and we have let God perform surgery on us and adjust some of our inside workings. Father does know best. If we've given the responsibility of our lives over to God then we have to trust that he is capable and willing to take on the responsibility to make decisions for our lives that are for our well-being. But when he makes those decisions, we have to choose to trust in his love and follow them—even if we can't see the end result which we usually don't.

It is not that we are blind; it is that God has allowed a fog to hamper the view of the future. Maybe he wants to see if we really do trust him …and he is asking will you follow me even if you don't know where I am leading you? Even if you can't see clearly the way in front of you? Even if you don't know "why"? It is not for us to understand God's doings, it only for us to obey God's commands. I have heard it said on many occasions that nothing is wasted in God's economy. We might not see the fruits of our actions when we submit to God's call, but God's ways are not our ways. And it is God's understanding that holds validity not ours. We can't count on ourselves to "get it." We can only count on God who has "got it" all. Trust and faith go hand in hand.

> Trust in the LORD with all your heart and lean not on your own understanding.
>
> Proverbs 3:5

When we trust God, we are putting faith into action. True faith is doing what God has called without knowing what will be on the other side of what we have been asked to do. Warren Wiersbe said, "Our faith is not really tested until God asks us to bear what seems unbearable, do what seems unreasonable, and expect what seems impossible."[12] Bentley trusts me and follows me wherever I go because she loves me. I feed her, I wash her, I play with her, and I teach her. I am her very best friend. Bentley might not understand reason, but she understands rewards; everything from a treat to a good scratch under the chin. And when she is asked to do something, she does it out of total love and devotion. She most always tries to comply. She came through the surgery without a glitch and happily is glad to be back in a familiar location with a familiar routine. She trusted me.

I know that it the same way God wants me to respond. Trust him. God does not have to reveal his intentions or his plan just as I don't have to do that with my children. I am called to trust him and have faith knowing that

God's target has been designated. His plan is in gear, and I am honored to be a servant in his kingdom. I might not understand his reasons, but I do understand his rewards for there is a surge of peace and contentment that resonates in my soul when I am following his lead.

God will test my faith ...on little things and on the big ones ...so for right now, maybe I should get into practice of submitting to God's will with his little things.

Dear Lord, it is not for me to ask you why or contemplate and try to pry. Just teach me to trust and obey your word, and let me absorb those things I've heard. I may not understand your way, but I am forever thankful you've come to stay. Amen.

Praise God wherever you are and whatever situation he has allowed you to be in. His glory will shine through!

approval
-november 7, 2007

Am I doing this right? I'm going on a gut instinct here. Is there something else I need to be doing to help Bentley? I called a professional trainer who came to my house a few weeks ago to take a look at Bentley. He watched her as she swam, as she fetched, as she walked, and as she struggled to get up on all fours. I *was* doing all that could be done except maybe putting her on a treadmill, but there was no guarantee that that would make any improvements. But as I was walking her tonight, I realized that one of his suggestions was right on target. He said before I praised her to make her stand up square, all four feet planted in their positions and then give her the much-loved scratch under the chin. I asked if I should give her a treat and he said, "*No,* dogs are quite content with your approval, and that is something that you will always have available not so with treats."

Bentley loves approval. Sometimes she just stops and stands square and waits for me to acknowledge that she has done a good job on her walk. Tonight was one of those nights. I had been busy all day, and she needed a little extra attention when we had made our way down the grassy path. Who could resist that precious face? Oh, and she tries so hard to do what is asked of her.

Where am I going with this? It is about approval. Are we content just knowing that we have God's approval when we have acted appropriately or followed his direction or allowed his guidance to forge our path? Or do we need an earthly treat or reward or confirmation to account for our productivity. I am one who is most guilty of this, especially with my family. I hate it that I want the recognition, but I am just like Bentley. I stand squarely in the face of my accomplishment and wait for recognition, and if by chance it goes unnoticed, seldom do I let it slide on by. I think of my husband, Mel, and how much he does around the house and for all of us and is hardly ever commended. He just goes about quietly, trucking on without need of acknowledgment. I want to be more like that!

Why isn't God's approval enough? I just figured it out. It is not the waiting for the response that is the issue it is the "who" I am waiting for the response from that causes the conflict. For if I am doing whatever I am doing unto the Lord and *not unto man,* knowing that it is pleasing to God, then the accolades that come from God will be the only ones who really matter because he will be the object of the intended task.

Am I now trying to win the approval of men, or of God? Or am I trying to please men? If I were still trying to please men, I would not be a servant of Christ.

Galatians 1:10

I am called to live my life for God not for man. Everything I do, everything I say, and all my thoughts are to be in line with what I have been taught through God's word. When I turn my focus to others and try to please them on all fronts, it just isn't going to happen. But if my efforts are focused on God and what he would have me do then I am at peace. I know that I have stayed the course and been faithful to the one who has created me, has walked beside me, has guided me, has loved me unconditionally. God has forgiven me, has a purpose for me, and has promised to *never* leave me. If I am faithful to God and to God's ways—the other things will just fall right into place!

> Whatever you do, work at it with all your heart, as working for the LORD, not for men.
>
> Colossians 3:23

As long as I can stand squarely in front of God, knowing that I have done my best for him and have asked forgiveness when I know I have blundered, then his approval and his encouragement will enfold my very being, and I will *know* in my soul that his grace and his mercy is upon me. Just as Bentley is so pleased with my approval, I too should be perfectly content with God's approval and not be needy of the approval of others. I am Bentley's trainer, her everyday buddy, her main caretaker. It makes sense that she wants my approval and also makes sense that she knows my commands and listens to my voice. She didn't choose me; I chose her (actually Molly did) and chose to keep her and love her and care for her. I do my best—most of the time; sometimes I slack off though and forget the walk or am late feeding her or not up to speed with the baths, but that doesn't make her any less devoted.

I think of God who chose me to be one of his children, to love me, and to care for me, he does his best all the time. He never slips up or is late in answering prayers or unfaithful to his promises, but how do I treat him? Am I devoted, truly devoted to him and responsive to his training? Maybe, just maybe, I ought to take a few lessons from Bentley. Seek approval from the one who loves you the most and be devoted and faithful and loyal, so loyal to the God who has cared for me throughout my lifetime. God has promised to never leave me or abandon me. God is the only true one I can depend on. He is caring for me in his right way everyday, and thankfully, he bases his actions on his instincts, for they are pure and worthy and true. If only I would respond to the lessons that my trainer is trying to teach me. Thankfully his approval is not based on my actions but on his love.

Dear Lord, let me absorb this lesson that you have given me through watching this precious dog. Let me be content with your approval and not seek the accolades of men. Let me do whatever I do unto you, knowing that if I am centered and focused on your and your ways. Then everything else will fall into the place that you have ordained. Amen.

Praise God wherever you are and whatever situation he has allowed you to be in. His glory will shine through!

scratch
-november 10 - 2007

Don't you just love it when you have an itch and you *can* get to it and scratch it? Have you ever had one you couldn't reach, and you have had to ask for a little help or it would drive you crazy? Well, I have realized that Bentley loves her neck to be scratched. It occurred to me one day that dogs scratch with their hind legs, and she doesn't have the muscle strength or coordination in those hind legs to be able to scratch. So, as often as I remember, I give Bentley a good scratch under her chin and on her stomach, and she stands perfectly square in complete appreciation for the gesture.

Have you been itching to do something lately? But for whatever the reason, you aren't able to get to it. Do you find that if you just keep on moving that it loses its impact? And sometimes if you give it your best shot to ignore it, the itch will finally fade away. But then what happens if it comes back again? You try the same defense, but this time to no avail. I think God has a way of putting these little discomforts and restless dreams upon us to get us thinking …thinking …*Maybe I should try this or maybe I should do that or pursue a dream or step our in faith toward something intriguing.* If God has put an itch on your mind and in your heart then pay attention to it. Scratching an itch is automatic, not something we think of and anticipate, just something we do.

As soon as we feel an itch, our first natural response is to scratch the spot of the itch with our fingernails. The reason for this response is simple—we want to remove the irritant as soon as possible. Once you've scratched the area of irritation, you are likely to feel some relief. When your brain realizes that you've scratched away the irritant, the signal being sent to your brain that you have an itch is interrupted and therefore no longer recognized by the brain.[13]

This is the same way it is with an itch that God gives us. He wants us to react to his itch with a natural response. He wants us to be so close to him that we recognize immediately when he is moving us through the sensations of our mind and heart. He sends us something that would just slightly rattle our comfort. Test the waters though and make sure the itch lines up with God's standards. Sometimes maybe we put *too* much thought into ideas or chores or dreams, and we beat them to pieces with so much thought that they never get off the ground … and the could of, should of, and would of …moment of opportunity and action are gone. If you have an itch, especially if you can't seem to reach it, let God give you the tools to scratch it. If he sends you an itch …and it lines up with his standards …*trust God.* Ask for his help and his direction and get ready! For just as Bentley is unable to scratch her itch, we too may be unable to scratch ours without God's help …and once we have chosen to accept his input …we are off!

I press on toward the goal to win the prize for which
God has called me heavenward in Christ Jesus.

Philippians 3:14

Be conscious of a sensation within your mind and heart
that says, "Go and do thus and so," or "Be faithful and
trust me as I send you to accomplish my desires," or "Step
out into new territory, for I have blessings for your there."
God is always willing to help you scratch the itch that he
instigates. Once you allow God to scratch the itch then
he has sent through *his* signal to *your* mind then the itch
has been interrupted, and you change the mind channel
of *scratch the itch* to *moving onward with the project* God
has submitted.

Dear Lord, sometimes we get stuck in the everyday
plain ole boxed up living. Free us from that and show
us that a little mind itch is often your way of getting
our attention and coercing us to pursue a new direction.
Sometimes it is in attitude; sometimes in action. When
you cause an itch, may we respond by asking for your help
to scratch. Let me be itching to do your will! Amen.

Praise God wherever you are and whatever situation *he*
has allowed you to be in. His glory will shine through!

bark

-november 27, 2007

I guess I hadn't thought too much about it. I probably would have been mad too! I was walking the dogs one night this week before lights out (about 10:00 p.m.), and we went our usual route, usual speed, usual exploring. On our way back one of my neighbors (who I do not know) came barreling out furious saying, "I have to talk to you!" She had her long terrycloth robe on, her purse anchored on her elbow, and a glass of ice water. Oh, she was mad! She said, "You walk your dogs in front of my house each night, and I don't know why, but you hang out in front of my house, and it makes my dog crazy. I have a seven-year-old and just quit walking past my house." She continued without a breathe, "You can walk past in the daytime, but please don't do it at night." I walk on Memorial, a busy public street. She has a large white *alpha male acting* German Shepherd. I know this because he got out once and chased us. He barks with a strong, loud-sounding cadence and keeps barking 'til you are out of sight. My dogs are quiet, so I guess he stands guard at the front window watching for them to pass by. Well, Bentley is a *slow* walker, and when she falls, it takes her a while to regroup and get her feet squared and keep on going. So when we pass her house, the dog's bark usually startles Bentley, causing her to fall, and you know the rest of the story.

"I'm so sorry; I won't come this way again." I explained Bentley's situation and that I was not "camping out" at her house, but that I *would* alter our route. I kept saying, "I am so sorry. I am so sorry." And I gathered my dogs and headed home.

So when was the last time someone barked at you? It is an awful feeling, and then I remembered I had just done the same thing to someone in defense of one of my children that same day! Thankfully, I handled it a little differently, but my emotions were in gear no doubt! I love that quote that says something like *watch out who you point the finger at because when you do there are three more pointing right back at you.* She was defending her seven-year-old's peacefulness. I'm sure she was annoyed as well, but that was her base line for the reprimand. I should have paid more attention and been aware of the barking dog, and the inconsideration I was showing, especially at nighttime, but when I walk the dogs, I am thinking about a bunch of other things and don't always pay close enough attention to what is around me.

Barking is just that. Barking. It is not gentle spirited. It is aggressive behavior that has no place in the behavior book of God's ways. Sure, it is fine to take issue with something, as a matter of fact, we probably need to be taking issue with a lot more than we do. We tend to look the other way and are afraid of confrontation when we know that things are not as they should be, afraid of offending someone who has a different viewpoint. But there are different ways of addressing conflict, and

God's way is through a loving heart. You can be stern and truthful without barking. I think there is a true art to it but we can accomplish it.

I don't know about you but most of the time when I finally hit frustration, it is hard to separate my emotions from my bark. The emotions are what get us in trouble because the emotions are reflected in the body language as well as the words, and they usually come untamed. So how do you tame a bark? With training, first recognize the bark is brewing, and then ask God to put the reigns on it: to calm down the wild urge to respond immediately, and to let the words that come out, come out with grace and composure. Figure out the real goal and stay focused. Emotions tend to get us going on a fast and uncontrolled barking battle, forgetting the real reason for the initial disruption. There are always regrets, even if you think you got them good with what you said. It only feels good for a minute, and then we start thinking, *I wish I would have just stayed quiet or spoken with control and gentleness, out of truth, not just to defend my position.* It is true. Big Bark. Big Bite. Soft Bark. God's Delight.

The quiet words of the wise are more to be heeded than the shouts of a ruler of fools.

Ecclesiastes 9:17

But really, I have seen how people who are really mad speak calmly and effectively and how effective that presence is. So often the bark is a release mechanism and not pursuant to a defined goal. If I could only remember to incorporate these lessons that God is showing me in my daily affairs, boy would my life be different.

Looking back, I will say God has made progress: my barking has been greatly tempered. I bet if you look back, you can see some changes too they are gradual, but God is working on all of us in his own time.

Dear Lord, thank you for helping me to see these three fingers pointing back at me. I am so often focused on what has been done to me rather than what I may be doing to someone else. Continue to put these lessons on my heart and not only make me mindful of them but also help me to apply them in all circumstances not just the ones that I choose. Amen.

Praise God wherever you are and whatever situation he has allowed you to be in. His glory will shine through!

accept

-november 20, 2007

She stands quietly at the door, looking in and waiting, and then she sees me coming. And she knows, and before she even sniffs it out, it is devoured. Bentley knows that each morning after breakfast is done that she and her friend, Khaki, get a breakfast treat. It is not some luscious surprise. It could be left over fruit or a stale muffin or a extra sausage. It doesn't matter. Bentley just knows that if we are giving it to her then it has got to be good, and she is mighty grateful for the offer. And I guess the attention as well.

Is God such our master that when he opens the doors and gives us something that we just accept it gladly and graciously without ponder or cautious pursuit? Do we truly believe that his gifts are all great? No matter how they are wrapped or at what time he chooses to present them! Oh, how I wish I could answer yes, but the truth is I do ask why? And I do analyze them! I am not as trusting and accepting as Bentley is because I know that some of the things that have been thrown my way have not always started out with a favorable taste. As a matter of fact, they have often been bitter, but I know I have been called to swallow them anyway and accept them as eventual nourishment for my soul.

Do you find yourself asking, when the door opens and a situation unfolds before you: Why is this here? Why now? What is God going to teach me? Can I return it to sender? Or are you like Bentley and just graciously take whatever God gives and wait patiently for the next offer. The thing about God is he doesn't give us leftovers or stale offerings that have been sitting on the shelf a while or unwanted overflow. God's gifts for us are personally chosen, freshly cultivated, and are distributed without waste. One of my favorite Bible stories, since I was a child, was the manna, heavenly bread, that would rain from the sky that God sent to his people in the wilderness each day. Just enough to fulfill their needs—no leftovers—and it was sent down fresh daily. Saving or storing it was not an option for this was a trust issue …and God would taint it and make it uneatable if they did try to save it (Exodus 16:13–20). I am so visual and to this day, the thought of the sight of bread coming from the sky is just so out there.

Bentley stands at the door with anxious anticipation waiting for her master (that would be me). Her desire is my presence and food not necessarily in that order. Simple stated that should be my desire: God's presence and his provisions. When I stand at the door and Bentley sees me, she comes running (or scooting I should say because of her weak leg) because she has associated the fact that if I am looking then I am getting ready to come out, and she doesn't want to miss the opportunity to greet me … what if I had treats?

Well, God does stand at our door each morning watching and waiting for us to get up and get going, but how often do I run to greet him in enthusiastic prayer, happy to be in his presence? Do I only pay attention to him because I think he might be giving out treats? Or do I truly desire to walk beside him throughout the day? Am I picky about what he offers? Do I only want to accept the offerings that I am familiar with and comfortable with or am I willing to try something new. God's blessings come fresh daily so no matter what I see or how I perceive it, if it is from God then it ultimately will be for my good!

Dogs are simple creatures; they love those who are their masters no matter what the temperament of the master, it is unconditional. They accept graciously whatever the master offers. They are compliant, eager, attentive, content, respectful, dependent, loyal, non-complaining, tail wagging by your side companions. Pretty commendable qualities and a devoted commitment that comes from a deep and heartfelt love. How do I treat my master, my God? Am I a compliant, eager, attentive, content, respectful, loyal, non-complaining, side-by-side companion whose devoted commitment comes from a deep and heartfelt love? I'm afraid not; I fall way short! Oh, I love God all right. But do I draw from that love and is that love the true source of my devotion, or do I try to do what is right when folks are looking and hope that is enough? Bentley sincerely is out to please *me*. I have to ask. Am I sincerely out to please *God?* I want to be!

Dear Lord, I know she is just a dog, but I want to be devoted to you as she is to me. I want to eagerly anticipate the time I get to spend with you each day and appreciate the little blessings as well as the grand ones. Make me attentive to your word and your call, Lord. Take away my complaining and help me to see the best that there is and trust you and the gifts you give. For you, Lord, are always right. You, Lord, are always good. And you, Lord, are always available. Whatever it is you choose for me to have is for a purpose that I might not know at the time but will trust that is for your good through me. Thank you for my daily provisions for they are personally chosen, freshly cultivated, and distributed without waste. Amen.

Praise God wherever you are and whatever situation he has allowed you to be in. His glory will shine through!

provisions
-february 4, 2008

It was six o'clock in the evening. I knew it because in the midst of kitchen conversation and distractions about, Bentley got up from her comfortable, settled in spot, walked to my feet, sat quietly, and, without a sound, looked up and stared intensely. It was dinnertime. And she wanted me to know that she knew the time had come. Animals do have a keen sense about schedules, especially if the routine doesn't vary too much, and ours doesn't. Breakfast at 7:00 a.m., dinner at 6:00 p.m. and bedtime at 10:00 p.m.!

As I looked at her, I wondered, *Is this the way I approach God with my needs?* Do I render myself free from distractions and quietly sit in his presence hoping that he will notice and eventually do something, or do I make some serious noise and beg for his attention and provision and action at that very moment. God knows when I come to him exactly why I have come. I don't need to say a word or give any explanation. Sometimes it is for comfort, sometimes for wisdom, and sometimes I just appreciate his honest, loyal, loving friendship. I know I can count on him in times of trouble, and in times of need no matter what his schedule or routine is he is always available.

Bentley came to *me,* even though there were several others in the kitchen because she knew I would recognize her request and would be the one to fulfill it. Are we in a spot where we truly know that we can go to God no matter what the issue it? It doesn't have to be a big off the chart deal; it can be something as little as which route should I take home. God knows our hearts and listens to each of our requests.

There have been times when I have begged for help and times when I have quietly just sat in God's presence waiting for his thoughts to be part of my thoughts. There have been times when I have been so frustrated with other people that I just needed him to settle my heart. And times when I have been so overjoyed by blessings that tears were rolling down my face. God knows all my sides and moods and all of my needs. He knows what makes me tick he knows what makes me sad and anxious and what sends a chill up my spine. He knows what will delight my soul and what to send (maybe something as small as an unexpected butterfly or rabbit darting across a yard) so that I will be reminded of his presence. If I would only be mindful, moment by moment, that whatever happens or is happening; God is beside me. Then I would never have to go at something or through something without knowing I can always appeal for his hand of direction, and it will be there.

Answer me when I call to you, O my righteous God. Give me relief from my distress; be merciful to me and hear my prayer.

Psalm 4:1

He can take it when I question what he has done or not done, for God knows what he does is for my best. I just so many times can't see it. God's schedule and timing are perfect for each of us. He knows just what we need and what we want, but often, what we want is not always what we need. God's schedule does vary. We don't understand his timing and cannot determine when and where or how he will choose to interact, but what we do know is that he sees us when we sit at his feet, and he knows why we have come and his provisions will always outshine our finite imaginings. We just have to continue to trust his ways and know that above all, he is the one to come to no matter what it is that we need. For he is a giving God a God of comfort, love, peace, grace, joy, and wisdom, and his ample supply of each of these never runs dry.

May your cup be filled and overflowing, and may you know that no matter how you go before God; whether you are rattling and shaking the gates of heaven pleading for mercy and grace or if you are coming pensive and solemn and heavy hearted, God sees you and knows you heart. He hears your voice and will answer the prayers you have submitted in his own way and in his own timing, but they will be answered!

Bentley sits waiting, but she sits knowing. May we be the same when we approach God.

Dear Lord, thank you for your daily provisions. Let us be mindful of this one day and be grateful for your presence in each of our lives. Let us not be so anxious for tomorrow to come that we do not seek your glory for this moment. You are a loyal and faithful God to be trusted and depended upon for our every concern. Blessed are we to be called your children. Amen.

Praise God wherever you are and whatever situation he has allowed you to be in. His glory will shine through!

be content
-march 12, 2008

Bentley had a bad sore on the bottom of her paw …so I took her to the vet. We got her some antibiotics, and the vet said to make sure to keep her paw bandaged and padded—especially before she goes on a walk. So for a few days I did just that. Bandaged and padded. Friday, was no different, I repeated the same routine (or so I thought), and replaced the bandages and padding on her foot. We then went walking. The next day when it was time for a walk, she couldn't stand up. I took the bandages off, looked at her paw, and it appeared to be slightly swollen …so I just left it uncovered. A few hours later, it had tripled in size. I soaked it and rubbed it and thought by morning it would have gone down. It hadn't. I took her to the emergency vet on Sunday, and there was nothing to be done except to keep massaging it. She told me to follow up with my regular vet on Monday because depending on the damage, she could lose her paw.

I had done this to this precious dog. I wrapped the bandages too tight, and it cut off the circulation—for a twenty-four hour period. She was in the vet for a week, as they tried to help her paw recover. Today she is home, her paw riddled with serious sores, and all I can do is pray to have her back, able to stand, and resuming her crippled walk. If only I could rewind …

Have you ever felt that way? I can't dwell on what has happened, for the past is just that ...*past* ...I only can look at what the situation is now and make the best out of it with God's help.

I tell you this story not to make you feel sorry for the dog or appreciate my guilt-ridden anxiety but as a reminder for all of us to be content with what we *do* have. Because so often, instead of being grateful for the situation that we do have, we pine for something more. And we forget to realize that whatever the situation is, it could be worse. Look around and you will see. I wanted God to heal Bentley and for her to be able to walk without limp or stress or tireless effort. And I tried to do my part, but even as good as my intentions were, they only made things worse. I made her stronger leg even weaker, and now we are back to the beginning, where she is *down* again.

God has a plan for this little, well not so little, dog. I must be patient and wait to see what he is going to do next. He will somehow work this into His good *again* ...but here are a few lessons that have been brought to mind:

1. Even though you do the best you can ...there are no guarantees that you are doing what you are doing right ...and you will make mistakes ...

Trust god with the outcome—

I have written you quite boldly on some points, as if to
remind you of them again, because of the grace God
gave me

Romans 15:15

2.   What is done is done …don't dwell on it …move on
and make the best out of what you've got
*When God forgives, he doesn't look back …he looks forward
to what is to come—*

Who is a God like you, who pardons sin and forgives
the transgression of the remnant of his inheritance? You
do not stay angry forever but delight to show mercy.

Micah 7:18

3.   Be content with what you have …it might not seem
all put together …and in order …but be thankful for
what you have …in this case …crippled is better than
not walking or being able to stand at all.
*God has allowed you to be in the position you are in for
his purpose—*

And we know that in all things God works for the good
of those who love him, who have been called according
to his purpose.

Romans 8:28

4.   When things seems blistered and out of sorts …look
for the positive …you sometimes will find it in the smile
of someone's face …I find a special encouragement for

recovery just by looking at the hope in Bentley's.
Seek God's face!

And without faith it is impossible to please God, because anyone who comes to him must believe that he exists and that he rewards those who earnestly seek him.

Hebrews 11:6

5.   Even in the midst of great turmoil …Bentley was grateful to be in her home spot …she knew she was loved and was being cared for.

Whatever turmoil is going on in your life …be grateful in your heart …that you are loved and cared for by God—

Cast all your anxiety on him because he cares for you.

1 Peter 5:7

6. You have to be patient and wait it out…. things will work out …but it will be God's way …and he does have something planned.

God knows the plans he has for you

Jeremiah 29:11

7. Unconditional love …it is seen in our pets …especially our dogs …even when we mess up big time!

Can you imagine the unconditional love that God has for each of us …and we are so undeserving …no matter what we do …he just keeps on loving us—

> Give thanks to the God of gods. His love endures forever.
>
> Psalm 136:2

Bentley could have lost her paw. That scare is over. Now we will wait to see what God has planned and what she will be able to do with it after this injury heals. I know that God cares even about a dog, and it just reminds me how much more he cares even about me.

I have signed a contract for *Raising* Bentley, hopefully to be released by Christmas ...and this devotional was not part of the original manuscript. I have a feeling that this was the lesson that God wanted me to conclude *Raising Bentley* with, and I am grateful that April, my editor, allowed me the courtesy to include it.

For it is about His overseeing mercy and his continued grace, and that is just the beginning of God's story!

Dear Lord, thank you for these lessons.... please keep sending them my way and help me to stand on the faith and the trust in you that I know to be true. You are a God of mercy and of love, and I am oh so grateful for your continued guidance that you send through your Holy Spirit. Bless Bentley. I know she is just a dog, but you have carried her this far, and she needs your continued help. Amen

Praise God wherever you are and whatever situation he has allowed you to be in. His glory will shine through!

afterward

Bentley was two years old in January of 2008. Her status, we believe, will probably remain much the same …two weak hind legs but an attitude of pure joy and delight. She may show a few improvements here and there but we are truly blessed for the progress she has maintained. .She wants to be able to stay up when she gets up, but her legs just kind of give way, especially if she in an excited mode and wants to go fast. Dr. Thorpe, our vet is just wonderful, and we are constantly trying new things …new bandages, new antibiotics, etc …but we have to face it …she has severely injured her spinal cord, and those nerves are not to be replaced. She just has to work around, and with, what she has. Bentley is tenacious, and she has a 'can do' spirit of joy, a sweet disposition and an appreciation for any affection that comes her way, including treats of all kinds.

Would I take on this challenge again? My answer would be, yes, but the rest of my family is not so nearly in love with her as I am. She has needed a tremendous amount of loving care, but to me, just seeing that precious smile and knowing that we saved her life is enough for me to hang on to. And to think that she *is* walking when there was only a slim five percent chance that she ever would …is totally God's grace and mercy. It might not be a pretty and normal gait …but she is up and on all fours.

As far as the stumbling, who of us ever stays on our feet all the time? Stumbling is just part of life! When I really stop and wonder if God is going to heal her, I think God must love it when people stop and stare as they see Bentley walk. For they always have such a look of compassion and feel so sorry for her, and then I say, "Oh, but she wasn't suppose to be alive much less able to walk, and God has answered our prayers. She is doing great." They sort of stand taller, exchange the sadness for a smile, begin to encourage Bentley, and then go about telling her what a great job she is doing.

Isn't that what we are to do for each other—look past our inadequacies and encourage one another? God has used this precious dog to teach me many a simple life lesson. I will be forever grateful for the answered prayers, though they were not the answers I had pictured; they were certainly the answers that drew a picture of courage, tenacity, and attitude from Bentley, my yellow, big-hearted lab friend and companion.

Bentley's paw has healed sufficiently, and she continues to be able to hop along with her back legs as she runs and plays. Either you focus on her handicap or you focus on her heart. She might be physically handicapped, but her heart is full of spirit and love, and she exudes a contented countenance of joy.

May some of these lessons be your lessons too, and may God bless you with his presence, comfort you in your afflictions, and give you a hope that is forever in your heart. For we all are handicapped in some way or another. Some of them are visible and some are not. It is not the handicap that defines us; it is how God equips us to live life through them that shows our character.

Thank you dear readers for taking the time to read through this story. My hope is that if you have never had a glimpse of how God works or how real he is that these stories of ordinary occurrences be a tiny shining light to help you to see Him, and know Him. May God bless you and may you, too, depend on Him when life throws you a head on, paralyzing situation, that you have no idea how to handle.

God is faithful, and you can count on Him to stay beside you no matter where you are or what is happening around you or within you. There is nothing too small or too big for God. He loves us, each of us and wants to be a part of our daily lives. He will not barge in though; he will wait for an invitation. Just ask God to come along side you, and I guarantee you, He will and your life will never ever ever be the same.

Praise God wherever you are and whatever situation he has allowed you to be in–For His Glory will shine through.

To God be the Glory!
TO GOD BE THE GLORY!

For Comments, questions, or contact information, please visit my website at www.cathyjodeit.com.

Thank you for choosing to pick up "Raising Bentley". May God's Blessings be upon you and his presence be beside you always! Cathy

end notes

1   Oswald Chambers, *My Utmost for His Highest*, (Grand Rapids, Discovery House, 1992).

2   Chuck Swindoll, *Growing Strong in the Seasons of Life*, (Multnomah Press, Portland, 1977).

3   Oswald Chambers, *My Utmost for His Highest*, (Grand Rapids, Discovery House, 1992).

4   Rich Mullins, Song "Sometimes by Step" *written originally by Beaker then verses were added by Rich Mullins (The World as Best as I Remember It, Volume Two*, 1991) (Franklin, TN: Reunion Records, 1991).

5   Oswald Chambers, *My Utmost for His Highest*, October 25 devotional (Grand Rapids, Discovery House, 1992).

CATHERINE JODEIT

6   Oswald Chamber, *"My Utmost for His Highest"*, January ninth, (Grand Rapids, Discovery House, 1992)

7   Wikipedia.com, s.v. "Clare Boothe Luce," "no good deed goes unpunished" unsourced, Wickipedia http://en.wikiquote.org/wiki/Clare_Boothe_Luce (accessed June 28, 2007).

8   Oswald Chambers, *"My Utmost for His Highest"*, June 27th, (Grand Rapids, Discovery House, 1992).

9   Chris Teagreen, *Why a Suffering World Makes Sense,* (Grand Rapids, Baker Books, 2006).

10   Tony Evans, *The Battle is the Lord's,* (Chicago: Moody Publishers, 1998).

11   Warren Wiersbe, "Faith being tested,", Sermons from the Book of Genesis, www.thelivingwordtbc.com/gen18.htm (accessed October 28, 2007).

12   How Stuff Works, "What is happening when you itch,", Body and Health, http, http://healthhowstuffworkscom/question600htm (question600htm (accessed November 10, 2007).